The Springer Series on Challenges in Machine Learning

Series editors

Hugo Jair Escalante, Puebla, Mexico
Isabelle Guyon, Berkeley, USA
Sergio Escalera, Barcelona, Spain

The books of this innovative series collect papers written by successful competitions in machine learning. They also include analyses of the challenges, tutorial material, dataset descriptions, and pointers to data and software. Together with the websites of the challenge competitions, they offer a complete teaching toolkit and a valuable resource for engineers and scientists.

More information about this series at http://www.springer.com/series/15602

Demian Battaglia · Isabelle Guyon
Vincent Lemaire · Javier Orlandi
Bisakha Ray · Jordi Soriano
Editors

Neural Connectomics Challenge

Foreword by Florin Popescu

 Springer

Editors
Demian Battaglia
Institute for Systems Neuroscience
University Aix-Marseille
Marseille
France

Isabelle Guyon
ChaLearn
Berkeley, CA
USA

Vincent Lemaire
Orange Labs
Lannion
France

Javier Orlandi
FMC Department
University of Barcelona
Barcelona
Spain

Bisakha Ray
NYU School of Medicine
New York, NY
USA

Jordi Soriano
FMC Department
University of Barcelona
Barcelona
Spain

ISSN 2520-131X   ISSN 2520-1328   (electronic)
The Springer Series on Challenges in Machine Learning
ISBN 978-3-319-85054-2   ISBN 978-3-319-53070-3   (eBook)
DOI 10.1007/978-3-319-53070-3

Foreword

Every year, thousands of scientists gather at one of the world's largest scientific conferences (Neuroscience) in which a casual visitor may be bewildered by the variety of competences, techniques, organisms, structures and behaviors studied and presented under one roof. Lost in the details, sometimes, is that the object of study is the same, one of the last great mysteries of nature: how does the brain work? Despite the breadth of the neuroscience community, progress has been relatively slow. Not every year is a sensational new advance presented in the community, which then spreads all over the globe and dominates future sessions and discussions. Two of the latest such advances are represented in this volume: the connectome (associated at first with diffusion MRI) and optical imaging (specifically calcium fluorescence imaging). Both techniques allow us to observe the large-scale structure of neuronal circuits and the brain with much higher spatial resolution than previous techniques. This duo has been joined lately by yet a third related technique, namely that of optical stimulation at fine scales, without contact and spatial resolution limitations of electrode and patch clamp preparations of old. Simultaneous optical imaging and stimulation, albeit with laborious preparation and strong caveats, has even been achieved in a live animal.

Insomuch as connectomics has been allegorically described (even before its inception) by Stanislav Lem's "Solaristics" these techniques are akin to actually having a space station orbiting Solaris rather than viewing it through distant telescopes. Yet we must ask ourselves, past the euphoria of having 'big neural data' at our disposal, what does optical imaging offer us in terms of addressing big picture questions that have not been addressable with older techniques, beyond an increased technical ability to test predictions of computational neuroscience at larger scales?

There is at least one relevant big picture item which has mystified neuroscientists for a long time, and even more as recent investigations show it is no recording artifact, as some skeptics claimed, but baffling reality. Given the high metabolic cost of the brain, and its tax on survival "in humans especially" why is it running at 95% capacity (energy and activity) when it is doing nothing compared to when it is busy in some mental task? Why is this true in primates, other organisms including *in vitro* self-assembled preparations, prenatally, in sleep and other seemingly idle states? What is the so-called default mode or idle state network up to? Would not the ability to image thousands or millions of neurons simultaneously and individually help answer this question better than low-resolution electrode arrays and BOLD imaging? More specifically, what is the relationship between frequency and spatial power laws of neural activity and how does it differ in idle vs. active states? How do predictions of various exotic theories on nonlinear dynamics in the brain and stability (meta-stability, strange attractors, spontaneous self-organization, fractal scaling, etc.) pan out? Finally, how are either these global behaviors related to functional connectivity?

It turns out that optical imaging has some limitations which would be difficult if not impossible to overcome experimentally, at least *in vivo*. First of all calcium channels and action potentials have low energy per neuron and millisecond: this must be so due to the scale involved. Any diversion from electrical energy to release of photons must also be small and probabilistic: optical imaging is therefore noisy. Furthermore, neurons lying in layers deeper with respect to the sensor are (partially) occluded. Reflection, refraction and absorption are expected: the signals are partial, under-sampled, aliased. The leverage we have to overcome this challenge is that with long enough recordings and transfer learning from experiment to experiment, we may use computer vision, machine learning and signal analysis methods to infer the functional and structural connectivity of the neural ensemble we are imaging. The task is quite complex, but we would not know how much information we can extract unless we test and push analytics methods to their limit. The volume represents a pioneering effort to construct a realistic simulation (actually a large set of simulations) which includes major recording limitations but features known ground truth, and a properly constructed method comparison process (in a data competition) which tests algorithms on unseen data, on unseen experiments. The results, bringing for the first time data scientists into the larger fold of neuroscience in the context of optical imaging, are surprisingly encouraging, and even more so since they did not explicitly require causal analysis of the networks seen. This is a very important and boldly pioneering effort in a portion of the community which is only likely to expand in the coming years.

Florin Popescu
Fraunhofer Institute for Open Communication
Systems FOKUS, Berlin, Germany

Preface

Neuroscience is nowadays one of the most appealing research fields for interdisciplinary research. The rich dynamics and complexity of living neuronal networks, and the brain in particular, has long fascinated biologists, physicists and mathematicians alike. In the last decade, however, and thanks to the giant development in computational tools and scientific interconnectivity through Internet, neuroscience has experienced a new drive that seems unstoppable and more interdisciplinary than ever.

Machine learning is one of the most innovative modern computational tools. In the context of neuroscience, it has already procured extraordinary results in brain activity data analysis, artificial intelligence, and human–machine interfacing. Machine learning tools have the capacity to predict the behavior or response of a complex system given sufficient data and training. This capacity is precisely what motivated us to launch the Connectomics Challenge. The task in mind was to solve an interesting yet highly complex inverse problem: given the time series of neuronal spontaneous activity, which is the underlying connectivity between the neurons in the network?

The present volume illustrates the efforts of the scientific community to use machine learning concepts to tackle this problem and to develop tools for the advancement of neuroscience. The volume is specially oriented to the mathematical, physical and computer science community that carries out research in neuroscience problems. It may also be of great interest for the machine learning community since it exemplifies how to approach the same problem from different perspectives. Finally, a broader readership may find interesting the description and development of the Connectomics Challenge itself and get a glimpse of major open problems in current neuroscience.

The contributions in this volume are organized as follows. Orlandi et al. will first provide an overview of the Connectomics Challenge, describing its goals, the procured data and challenge development, to finally compare the strategies and outcome among participants. The next five articles will describe in detail different approaches used by the participants to tackle the problem. They include partial correlation analysis by Sutera et al.; a connectivity feature engineering pipeline by

Magrans et al.; a convolutional approach by L. Romaszko; the use of Csisz's Transfer Entropy and regularization by Tao et al.; and a random forest classification algorithm by Czarnecki et al. The next two contributions close the volume by illustrating the potential of machine learning approaches to support neuroscience research. Ma et al. will describe a Poisson Model to infer spikes trains from in vivo recordings in the rat brain; and Laptev et al. will introduce a neuroimage tool to enhance information retrieval from image sequences and apply it to improve neuronal structure segmentation.

Marseille, France   Demian Battaglia
Berkeley, USA   Isabelle Guyon
Lannion, France   Vincent Lemaire
Barcelona, Spain   Javier Orlandi
New York, USA   Bisakha Ray
Barcelona, Spain   Jordi Soriano
April 2015

Contents

First Connectomics Challenge: From Imaging to Connectivity

**Javier Orlandi, Bisakha Ray, Demian Battaglia, Isabelle Guyon,
Vincent Lemaire, Mehreen Saeed, Alexander Statnikov, Olav Stetter
and Jordi Soriano**

*Editors: Demian Battaglia, Isabelle Guyon, Vincent Lemaire,
Javier Orlandi, Bisakha Ray, Jordi Soriano*

Abstract We organized a Challenge to unravel the connectivity of simulated neuronal networks. The provided data was solely based on fluorescence time series of spontaneous activity in a network constituted by 1000 neurons. The task of the participants was to compute the effective connectivity between neurons, with the goal to reconstruct as accurately as possible the ground truth topology of the network. The procured dataset is similar to the one measured in in vivo and in vitro recordings of calcium fluorescence imaging, and therefore the algorithms developed by the participants may largely contribute in the future to unravel major topological features of living neuronal networks from just the analysis of recorded data, and without the

The original form of this article appears in JMLR W&CP Volume 46.

J. Orlandi (✉) · J. Soriano
Departament de Física de la Matèria Condensada, Universitat de Barcelona, Barcelona, Spain
e-mail: orlandi@ecm.ub.edu

J. Soriano
e-mail: jordi.soriano@ub.edu

B. Ray (✉) · A. Statnikov
Center for Health Informatics and Bioinformatics, New York University Langone
Medical Center, New York, NY, USA
e-mail: bisakha.ray@nyumc.org

A. Statnikov
e-mail: alexander.statnikov@nyumc.org

D. Battaglia
Institute for Systems Neuroscience, Aix-Marseille University, Marseille, France
e-mail: demian.battaglia@univ-amu.fr

D. Battaglia · O. Stetter
Bernstein Center for Computational Neuroscience, Göttingen, Germany

need of slow, painstaking experimental connectivity labeling methods. Among 143 entrants, 16 teams participated in the final round of the challenge to compete for prizes. The winners significantly outperformed the baseline method provided by the organizers. To measure influences between neurons the participants used an array of diverse methods, including transfer entropy, regression algorithms, correlation, deep learning, and network deconvolution. The development of "connectivity reconstruction" techniques is a major step in brain science, with many ramifications in the comprehension of neuronal computation, as well as the understanding of network dysfunctions in neuropathologies.

Keywords Neuronal networks · Effective connectivity · Fluorescence calcium imaging · Reconstruction · Graph-theoretic measures · Causality

1 Introduction

All living neuronal tissues, from the smallest in vitro culture up to the entire brain, exhibit activity patterns that shape the modus operandi of the network. Activity may take the form of spontaneous discharges, as occurs in the absence of stimuli, or in the form of precise patterns of activity during information processing, memory, or response to stimuli. A major paradigm in modern neuroscience is the relation between the observed neuronal activity (function) and the underlying circuitry (structure). Indeed, activity in a living neuronal network is shaped by an intricate interplay between the intrinsic dynamics of the neurons and their interconnectivity throughout the network.

In the quest for understanding the structure-function relationship, the neuroscience community has launched a number of endeavors which, in an international and cooperative effort, aim at deciphering with unprecedented detail the structure of the brain's circuitry (connectome) and its dynamics (Kandel et al. 2013; Yuste and Church 2014). In Europe, the Human Brain project aspires at developing a large-scale computer simulation of the brain, taking advantage of the plethora of data that is continuously being

I. Guyon
ChaLearn, Berkeley, CA, USA
e-mail: guyon@chalearn.org

V. Lemaire
Orange Labs, Lannion, France
e-mail: vincent.lemaire@orange.com

M. Saeed
National University of Computer and Emerging Sciences, Lahore, Pakistan
e-mail: mehreen.saeed@nu.edu.pk

O. Stetter
Max Planck Institute for Dynamics and Self-Organization, Göttingen, Germany
e-mail: olav@nld.ds.mpg.de

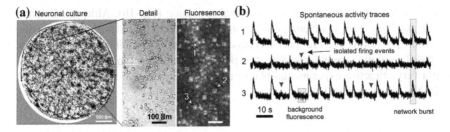

Fig. 1 Experimental motivation. **a** Example of a neuronal culture, derived from a rat embryonic cortex and containing on the order of 3000 neurons. The detail shows a small area of the network in bright field and fluorescence, depicting individual neurons. In a typical experiment, neurons are identified as regions of interest (*yellow boxes*), and their analysis provide the final fluorescence times series to be analyzed. **b** Fluorescence spontaneous activity traces for 3 representative neurons. Data are characterized by a background signal interrupted either by episodes of coherent activity termed *network bursts*, or by individual firing events of relative low amplitude and occurrence (color figure online)

gathered. In the United States, the BRAIN Initiative aims at developing technologies to record neuronal activity in large areas of the brain, ultimately linking single-cell dynamics, connectivity, and collective behavior to comprehend brain's functionality. The difficulty and high cost of these quests (Grillner 2014) have called for parallel, more accessible strategies that can complement these large-scale projects.

With the hope to delineate parallel strategies in the understanding of neuronal circuits, we launched in April 2014 a 'Connectomics Challenge' aimed at developing computational tools to answer a simple yet defying question: how accurately can one reconstruct the connectivity of a neuronal network from activity data? To shape the challenge, we built a numerical simulation in which we first designed a neuronal circuit, therefore establishing its ground–truth topology, and later simulated its dynamics considering neurons as leaky integrate-and-fire units. We also modeled the recording artifacts and noise associated with calcium imaging.

The network that we simulated mimics the spontaneous activity observed in neuronal networks in vitro. Neuronal cultures, i.e. neurons extracted from brain tissue and grown in a controlled environment (Fig. 1a), constitute one of the simplest yet powerful experimental platforms to explore the principles of neuronal dynamics, network connectivity, and the emergence of collective behavior (Eckmann et al. 2007; Wheeler and Brewer 2010). The relative small size of these networks, which typically contain a few thousand neurons, allows for the monitoring of a large number of neurons or the entire population (Spira and Hai 2013; Orlandi et al. 2013; Tibau et al. 2013). The subsequent data analysis —often in the context of theoretical models— provides the basis to understand the interrelation between the individual neuronal traces, neuronal connectivity, and the emergence of collective behavior. Activity in cultures can be recorded by a number of techniques, from direct electrical measurements (Spira and Hai 2013) to indirect measurement such as fluorescence calcium imaging (Grienberger and Konnerth 2012; Orlandi et al. 2013), which uses the influx of Calcium upon firing to reveal neuronal activation (Fig. 1b). Although Calcium imaging has a typical temporal resolution on the order of ms, its non-invasive nature and the possibility to simultaneously access a large number of neurons with accurate spatial resolution (only limited by the optical system for measurements) have made it a very attractive experimental platform both in vitro and in vivo (Bonifazi et al. 2009; Grewe et al. 2010).

2 Challenge Design

The goal of the Challenge was to identify directed connections of a neuronal network from observational data. Using this kind of data constitutes a paradigm shift from traditional approaches based on interventional data and causal inference, where a planned experiment is required to perturb the network and record its responses. Although interventional approaches are required to unambiguously unravel causal relationships, they are often costly and many times technically impossible or unethical. On the other hand, observational data, which means recordings of an unperturbed system, can be used to study much larger systems and for longer periods.

The data for the challenge was generated using a simulator previously studied and validated (Stetter et al. 2012; Orlandi et al. 2014) for neuronal cultures. As shown in Fig. 1, mature neuronal cultures usually develop into a bursting regime, characterized by long periods of very low neuronal activity and short periods of very high (bursting) activity (Orlandi et al. 2013; Tibau et al. 2013). This is a very interesting regime to check connectivity inference algorithms, since the system switches from a scenario where connections play almost no role to another one where the system appears to be highly coherent with effective all-to-all connectivity profiles (Stetter et al. 2012). Although these two dynamic states shape different effective connectivities, the actual structural connectivity layout remains unchanged.

Connectivity inference techniques have usually focused on analyzing spiking data, with binary signals identifying the presence (1) or absence (0) of neuronal firing. However, real spiking data are only available for a narrow set of experimental systems, and usually involve invasive electrode arrays or single-cell (path clamp) techniques. Recent advances in imaging allow the simultaneous recording of thousands of neurons (Ohki et al. 2005; Panier et al. 2013). However, the identification of single spikes in imaging data cannot always be accomplished and one has to directly analyze the fluorescence signals. Our data also take that into account and the signal given to participants models the fluorescence signal of a calcium marker activated when a neuron fires. It also takes into account most of the experimental limitations, such as low acquisition speed, noisy data, and light scattering artifacts (Stetter et al. 2012). The latter is important, since the fluorescence of a neuron influences the neighboring ones, giving rise to correlations between signals that are spurious.

The major features of the simulated networks for the Challenge are the following:

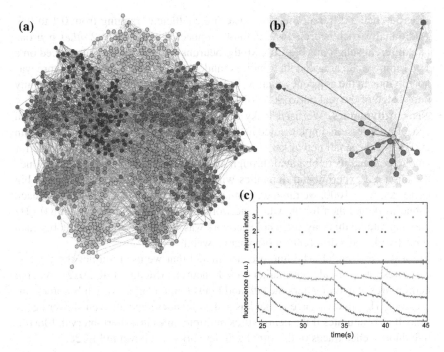

Fig. 2 Simulated neuronal network for the Challenge. **a** The designed network contained 1000 neurons preferentially connected within 10 communities (marked with different colors in the figure), and with additional connections between communities. Each neuron connected on average with 30 other neurons. **b** A detail of the connections of a single neuron. For clarity, only 50% of the connections are shown. **c** *Top* Raster plot showing the spontaneous activity of 3 randomly chosen neurons in the network. *Bottom* Corresponding fluorescence traces. Note the existence of both network bursts and isolated firings. Traces are vertically shifted for clarity (color figure online)

- **Network structure**. Our simulated data is inspired on experimental recordings in an area of roughly $1 \, mm^2$ (Stetter et al. 2012; Tibau et al. 2013). In that region all neurons are able to physically reach any other neuron and the network can be considered as a random graph. For the small training datasets we used $N = 100$ neurons with an average connectivity of $\langle k \rangle = 12$ and varying levels of clustering,[1] from 0.1 to 0.6, and the neurons were placed randomly in a 1×1 mm square area (Guyon et al. 2014). For the larger datasets however, we used a different network structure that was never revealed to the participants. This network is shown in Fig. 2a, and its *reconstruction* by the participants shaped the overall goal of the challenge. Those datasets (including the ones used for the final scores) consisted of $N = 1000$ neurons. The neurons were distributed in 10 subgroups of different sizes, and each neuron connected with other neurons in the same subgroup with the same probability, yielding an *internal* average connectivity of $\langle k_i \rangle = 10$. Each

---

[1]Understood as the "average clustering coefficient" in network theory, i.e. the number of triangles a neuron forms with its neighbors over the total number of triangles it could form given its connectivity.

subgroup had a different internal clustering coefficient, ranging from 0.1 to 0.6. Additionally, each neuron was randomly connected with $\langle k_o \rangle = 2$ *other* neurons of a different subgroup (Fig. 2b). All the neurons were then randomly placed on a 1×1 mm square area and their indices randomized, so the network structure was not obvious in the adjacency matrix. In fact, none of the participants reported any knowledge of the real network topology.

- **Neuron dynamics**. We used leaky integrate and fire neurons with short term synaptic depression, implemented in the NEST simulator (Gewaltig and Diesmann 2007). For the small networks, $N = 100$, the synaptic weights were the same for any neuron and were obtained through an optimization mechanism to reproduce the observed experimental dynamics with a bursting rate of 0.1 Hz. For the big networks, $N = 1000$, we ran the optimization mechanism independently for each subnetwork and then for the whole network to also achieve the target of a 0.1 Hz bursting rate. In this way, the whole network was bursting as a single unit, but each subnetwork had a different set of synaptic weights.
- **Fluorescence model**. The fluorescence model that we used mimics the fluorescence response of calcium markers inside neurons (Stetter et al. 2012). When a neuron fires, calcium enters the cell and binds to the marker, which becomes fluorescent. This fluorescence signal has a slow response and an even slower decay time. It also saturates if the neuron fires multiple times in a short interval. Illustrative fluorescence traces of the simulated networks are shown in Fig. 2c.

The network architectures used to generate the simulated data are summarized in Table 1.

3 Results

The challenge lasted three months (from February 5 to May 5, 2014) and attracted 143 participants. The participants were asked to work simultaneously in two equivalent datasets, one for validation of the 'reconstruction' code and one for actual testing. They received immediate feed-back on the validation dataset on a public leaderboard. On the test dataset, however, their scores remained hidden until the end of the challenge. The scores from the private leaderboard (calculated on test data) for the top ten ranking participants are shown in Table 2. The calculated metric is the 'area under the curve' (AUC) of a *Receiver-Operator Characteristic* (ROC)[2] analysis (Bradley 1997; Stetter et al. 2012), a metric commonly used in classification problems. Here, we brought back the problem of network reconstruction to a two-class classification problem: edge present or absent. The motivation for using this metric is its availability on the Kaggle platform used for the challenge and its familiarity to challenge participants. In Sect. 3.3, we compare this metric with the area under the *Precision Recall* (PR) curve, a metric often used in information retrieval, which could be used as an alternative scoring method.

---

[2]The AUC is computed by integrating the ROC curve.

Table 1 Data procured to the participants. Each archive contained files with the fluorescence time series (F) and the spatial location of the neurons (P). The adjacency matrix (N) was also provided in the archives used for training purposes

Archive	Description	Provided files
validation	Fluorescence and positional data for the validation phase of the challenge (results on 'public leaderboard'). Network of N = 1000 neurons	F, P
test	Fluorescence and positional data for the test phase of the challenge (results on 'private leaderboard'). Network of N = 1000 neurons	F, P
small	Six small networks with N = 1000 neurons. Each network has the same connectivity degree but different levels of clustering coefficient, intended for fast checks of the algorithms	F, P, N
normal-1	Network of N = 1000 neurons constructed similarly to the 'validation' and 'test' networks	F, P, N
normal-2	Network of N = 1000 neurons constructed similarly to the 'validation' and 'test' networks	F, P, N
normal-3	Network of N = 1000 neurons constructed similarly to the 'validation' and 'test' networks	F, P, N
normal-3-highrate	Same architecture as normal-3, but with highly active neurons, i.e. higher firing frequency	F, P, N
normal-4	Network of N = 1000 neurons constructed similarly to the 'validation' and 'test' networks	F, P, N
normal-4-lownoise	Same network architecture as normal-4 (and same spiking data) but with a fluorescence signal with a much better signal to noise ratio	F, P, N
highcc	Network of N = 1000 neurons constructed similarly to the 'validation' and 'test' networks, but with a higher clustering coefficient on average	F, P, N
lowcc	Network of N = 1000 neurons constructed similarly to the 'validation' and 'test' networks, but with a lower clustering coefficient on average	F, P, N
highcon	Network of N = 1000 neurons constructed similarly to the 'validation' and 'test' networks, but with a higher number of connections per neuron on average	F, P, N
lowcon	Network of N = 1000 neurons constructed similarly to the 'validation' and 'test' networks, but with a lower number of connections per neuron on average	F, P, N

The results of the top ranking participants who submitted their code were verified by the organizers, who successfully reproduced their results. These results and pointers to code are shown in Appendix A. The second ranked participants chose not to submit their code and renounced to their prize.

Table 2 Private leaderboard rankings for the top 10 participants (test AUC scores)

#	Team name	Score
1	AAAGV	0.94161
2	Matthias Ossadnik	0.94102
3	Ildefons Magrans	0.94063
4	Lukasz 8000	0.93956
5	Lejlot and Rafal	0.93826
6	Sium	0.93711
7	Alexander N and Vopern	0.93666
8	Gaucho 81	0.93385
9	Killertom	0.93011
10	Dhanson	0.92885

We also surveyed the participants to compile statistics about algorithm, software and hardware usage, as well as human and computer time spent[3] Below we provide some general analyses of the results of the competition.

3.1 Challenge Duration

The graph in Fig. 3 shows performance progression as a function of time. We have plotted the best public and private AUC submitted for each day versus the number of days from the beginning of the challenge. Two baseline performances of GTE and correlation with discretization have also been added. The performances increased slowly throughout the challenge, but most notably in the first two months. However, the survey indicates that only one third of the participants estimated that they had sufficient time to complete the tasks of the challenge. One third also expressed their interest to continue refining the methods.

The graph in Fig. 4 shows the number of submissions above baseline. The vertical red and green lines are the AUCs using baseline techniques GTE and correlation with discretization. Out of 1827 total submissions received, 321 were invalid submissions (AUC = 0.0), 106 had an AUC below 0.5, 116 had an AUC between 0.5 and 0.68946 (the first baseline 'correlation with discretization'), 527 have an AUC between 0.68946 and 0.89252 (the second baseline 'GTE'), and 767 had an AUC above GTE. The median value of all the submissions (with an AUC above 0.5) was 0.89905.

---

[3]http://tinyurl.com/connectomicsDatasheet.

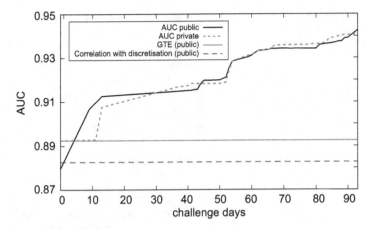

Fig. 3 Progression of the average performance of the participants along the duration of the challenge, comparing the AUC results on the validation dataset (public) with the results on the test dataset (private). The *blue* and *dashed red lines* indicate baseline techniques, and correspond to GTE and correlation with discretization AUCs, respectively (color figure online)

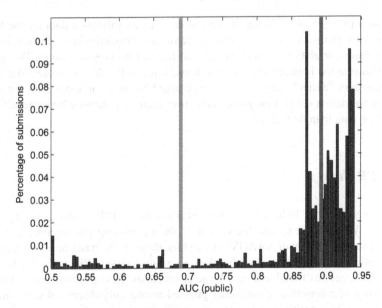

Fig. 4 Histogram of all the submissions received during the challenge. The *green* and *red bars* indicate baseline techniques, and correspond to GTE and correlation with discretization, respectively (color figure online)

Fig. 5 Scatter plot of
validation versus test AUC
scores for the top participants

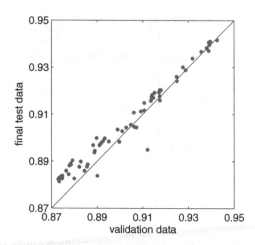

3.2 Overfitting

The graph in Fig. 5 plots the results on test data *versus* validation data for the final
submissions, limited to scores exceeding the results obtained with plain correlation
(i.e. Pearson correlation coefficient with no lag and no preprocessing). We see a
strong correlation between the validation and test results. At low scores, the final
test data seem "easier" (larger scores are obtained by most participants on test data
than on validation data). Few participants overfitted by obtaining better results on
validation data than on test data.

3.3 PR Curves

First, we compared ROC curves and precision-recall (PR) curves, as depicted
in Fig. 6. We show in orange the curves of the top ranking participants, in black
those of the winner (team AAAGV) and in blue those of the baseline method based
on Transfer Entropy. We remind that the true positive ratio (TPR) is the fraction of
correct connections found among all true connections, false positive ratio (FPR) is
the fraction of connections erroneously guessed among truly absent links, "recall" is
a synonym of true positive ratio and "precision" is the fraction of correct connections
found among all connections called significant.

In many ways the PR curve is more useful for experimentalists to assess the
accuracy of the networks. For instance, using the green curve, we can see that, if
we are willing to accept that 50% of the connections are wrong (precision of 0.5),
we can retrieve 40% of the connections of the network (recall or TPR of 0.4). In
contrast, the readings of the ROC curve may be deceivingly good: for a TPR of

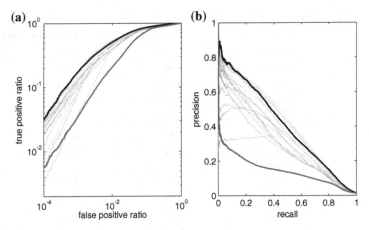

Fig. 6 Performance of the Challenge winner (AAAGV team, shown in *black*), the rest of participants (*orange*), and the performance procured by Transfer Entropy (*blue*) with two classical benchmarks: **a** Receiver operating characteristic (ROC) curve and **b** precision recall curve (color figure online)

0.4 ($\log 10(0.4) \simeq -0.4$), we obtain an FPR in 0.01, but, we care much less about correctly identifying absent connections than missing true connections.

3.4 Edge Orientation

Another important aspect of the problem we posed is the capability of network reconstruction algorithms to identify the direction of the connection, not only the presence or absence of a connection. Our metric of success did not emphasize connection orientation, making it possible to obtain good results even with a symmetric matrix. To separate the algorithms with respect to edge orientation, we computed the score of the challenge (AUC) limited to the pairs of neurons having only one connection in either direction ("connected neurons"). The results are shown in Table 3. It illustrates that edge orientation is very difficult compared to merely detecting the presence of a connection: the best score drops from 0.94 for the undirected network to 0.64 for the directed one. Team ranked number 4 (Lukasz 8000) performed best with respect to this metric. This team used a deep learning method based on convolutional neural networks. Feature learning may have played an important role in detecting details of the time series that are useful to determine edge orientation.

3.5 Subnetworks

Unknown to the participants, the large networks that we used for validation and test data had a substructure: they were organized in 10 subnetworks with varying

Table 3 Analysis of edge orientation (AUC scores)

#	Team name	Undirected network	Directed network
1	AAAGV	0.94	0.61
2	Matthias Ossadnik	0.94	0.63
3	Ildefons Magrans	0.94	0.60
4	Lukasz 8000	0.94	0.64
5	Lejlot and Rafal	0.94	0.63
6	Sium	0.94	0.63
7	Alexander N and Vopern	0.94	0.61
8	Gaucho 81	0.93	0.61
9	Killertom	0.93	0.61
10	Dhanson	0.93	0.61
Mean		0.94	0.62

Fig. 7 AUC scores of subnetworks (averaged over the top ten ranking participants) as a function of clustering coefficient, drawn in log scale for clarity

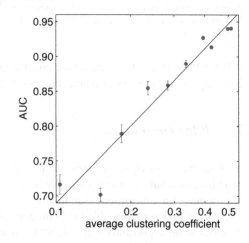

clustering coefficients. We define the clustering coefficient as the average over the sub-network of local clustering coefficients. Local clustering coefficients (Watts and Strogatz 1998) compute the ratio of connected neighbors of a node over the total number of possible connections. In Fig. 7 we show that the AUC scores of subnetworks (averaged over the top ten ranking participants) vary linearly with the log of the average clustering coefficients of the subnetworks.

We also computed the "long range" AUC score, i.e. the AUC score restricted to connections between subnetworks. On average over all top 10 ranking participants we obtained 0.8 (compared to 0.94 for the overall network).

4 Methods

For each category of methods (pre-processing, feature selection, dimensionality reduction, classification etc.) we report the fraction of participants having used each method. Note that the sum of these numbers do not necessarily add up to 100%, because the methods are not mutually exclusive and some participants did not use any of the methods.

The algorithmic steps for network reconstruction could be very broadly divided into the following steps:

1. **Preprocessing of fluorescence signals**: Figure 8a summarizes the different pre-processing techniques used by the participants. Some of the methods of the participants were spike timing extraction using either filtering and thresholding techniques, or through deconvolution methods such as (Vogelstein 2009; Vogelstein et al. 2009).
2. **Feature extraction**: Figure 8b shows the different feature extraction techniques used by the participants. Inverse correlation was used to filter out indirect interactions via fast partial correlations (Ryali et al. 2012).
3. **Dimensionality reduction**: The statistics in terms of number and percentage of participants for the different techniques used for dimensionality reduction is shown in Fig. 8c.

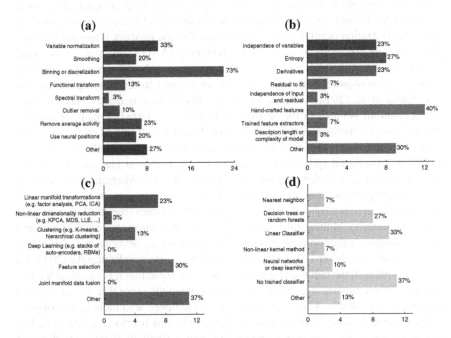

Fig. 8 Summary of the different methods used by the participants. *Bars* represent total count, and percentages the fraction of participants that used each method. **a** Preprocessing of fluorescence signals. **b** Feature extraction. **c** Dimensionality reduction. **d** Classification techniques

4. **Classification techniques**: Some recurrent techniques used by the participants were deep learning (Weston et al. 2012), generalizations of transfer entropy (Barnett et al. 2009; Orlandi et al. 2014) and information theoretical features, ad hoc topological features (e.g. geometric closure) and growing "a lot of trees" (random forests (Breiman 2001), boosting methods). The statistics in terms of number and percentage of participants for the different techniques used for classification are shown in Fig. 8d.

We also analyzed the factsheets with respect to the hardware and software implementations:

- **Hardware**: Many participants made use of parallel implementations (80% used multiple processor computers and 13% ran analyses in parallel). Memory usage was substantial (50% used less than 32 GB and 27% less than 8 GB).
- **Software**: Most participants used Linux (50%), followed by Windows (40%) and MAC OS (30%). Python was the top choice (67%) for coding, followed by MATLAB (37%).

The amount of human effort involved in adapting the code to the problems of the challenge varied but was rather significant because about 37% of the participants reported spending more than two weeks of programming. The total machine effort varied, with 43% reporting more than a few hours while another 27% reported more than two weeks.

A brief description of the methods of the top four ranking participants is given in the Appendix. Common to all method was the importance of preprocessing, including signal discretization or inference of spike trains. But the network inference step was rather different in the various methods. The winners (AAAGV) inferred an undirected network obtained through partial correlations, estimated with inverse covariance matrix, then post-processed the network in an attempt to recover edge directions (see Sutera et al. (2014) for details). Hence this method is multivariate: it takes into account all neurons in the network, it is not solely based on pairs of neurons like the baseline method used in Generalized Transfer Entropy. Matthias Ossadnik (ranked second) used a different multivariate approach: he used multivariate logistic regression of inferred spike trains, followed by an AdaBoost classifier integrating other information, including neuronal firing rates. Ildefons Magrans (ranked third) used multiple pairwise connectivity indicators varying the preprocessing parameters, integrated by an overall classifier based on ensembles of trees (see de Abril and Nowe (2014) for details). Multivariate interactions were taken into account in that method by post-processing the connectivity matrix with network deconvolution. Lukasz 8000 (ranked fourth) used deep convolutional neuronal networks (see Romaszko (2014) for details). Although the method is sophisticated in the sense that it is based on learned features of the temporal signal, it is not multivariate in the sense that it treats pairs of neurons independently. The proceedings of the challenge also include descriptions of the method of team Lejlot and Rafal (Czarnecki and Jozefowicz 2014), ranked 5, using several based predictors integrated with a Random Forest classifier and the method of killertom (Tao et al. 2014), ranked 9, using an improved version of Generalized Transfer Entropy (which was given as baseline method).

It is promising to see that several of the top ranking participants obtained good performance based only on statistics of pairs of neurons. Although clearly multivariate methods should provide superior performance, pairwise methods promise to scale much better to larger networks.

5 Conclusions

This first connectomics challenge allowed us to identify state-of-the-art methods to solve a difficult network reconstruction problem. The methods of the top ranking participants were very diverse and will pave the way to further research, integrating key ideas and analysis tools to increase performance. The participants performed better on the problem of edge detection than on edge orientation. More emphasis should be put on orientation in upcoming challenges. In the future we intend to involve both the challenge organizers and the participants in a deeper analysis of the devised strategies and analysis tools. We are also in the process of applying the methods of the top ranking participant to real biological data to assess their ability to reveal or predict key connectivity features of living neuronal networks. In collaboration with biologists, we are also preparing new data for a future connectomics challenge dedicated to the analysis of in vivo and in vitro recordings.

Acknowledgements This challenge is the result of the collaboration of many people. We are particularly grateful to our advisors and beta-testers who contributed to the challenge website and/or to review this manuscript: Gavin Cawley, Gideon Dror, Hugo-Jair Escalante, Alice Guyon, Sisi Ma, Eric Peskin, Florin Popescu, and Joshua Vogelstein. The challenge was part of the WCCI 2014 and ECML 2014 competition programs. Prizes were donated by Microsoft. The challenge was implemented on the Kaggle platform, with funds provided by the EU FP7 research program "Marie Curie Actions". This work used computing resources at the High Performance Computing Facility of the Center for Health Informatics and Bioinformatics at the NYU Langone Medical Center.

Appendix A. Challenge Verification Results

1. **Winners prize #1 (first place, verified) 500 USD and 1000 USD travel award + Award certificate**

   AAAGV

   The code from the winning team AAAGV, publicly available at https://github.com/asutera/kaggle-connectomics, was run successfully on a desktop PC, it used 7 GB of RAM and it took 30 h to run in single core mode on a 3 GHZ i7 CPU for each dataset. The code is built in Python and only uses standard dependencies. There was a issue with a specific library version but this has been resolved. Also we only need to run 1 script for the whole computation (main.py). From the valid dataset we obtained an AUC of 0.9426 and for the valid dataset and 0.9416 for the test dataset, which are the same as the ones reported in Kaggle.

2. **Winners prize #2 (third place, verified) 250 USD and 750 USD travel award + Award certificate**

   Ildefons

   The code from Ildefons team is publicly available at https://github.com/ildefons/ connectomics and consists of 6 separate scripts. The following are the time and memory requirements for each of the scripts. The main challenges were installing the required R package gbm and his script makeFeatures.R which needed 128 G. This R script started a MATLAB server in the SGE (Sun Grid Engine) background. We had to execute makeFeatures.R separately for normal-1, normal-2, valid, and test. His code was executed on the standard compute nodes on the cluster. The compute nodes have 2 INTEL CPUs, 16 processing cores, and 128 GB RAM. The statistics for the execution of his code can be found in Table 4.

   The code passed verification successfully. His AUC for the Kaggle submission generated by us is 0.94066. This is better than his leader board score of 0.93900. The difference between the two scores is 0.00166.

3. **Winners prize #3 (fourth place, verified) 100 USD and 400 USD travel award + Award certificate**

   Lukasz Romaszko

   The code for Luaksz Romaszko team can be obtained at https://github.com/ lr292358/connectomics. The details for Lukasz's code can be found in Table 5. His solution involved predicting the outcomes eight different times and averaging. All of his code passed verification successfully. The bottlenecks were installing theano (Python module) on the GPU units and gaining access to the GPU units. We have 5 cluster nodes with GPU accelerators. Each node has 1 accelerator. Each GPU has 2496 cores. The accelerator is NVIDIA Tesla Kepler (K20).

   After merging, his score is 0.93931, which is slightly better than his score of 0.93920 on the leader board. The difference between the two is 0.00011 or, in other words, negligible.

Appendix B. Description of Sample Methods and Sample Code

Matlab: We provide Matlab sample code to:

- read the data
- prepare a sample submission
- visualize data
- compute the GTE Stetter et al. (2012) coefficient and a few other causal direction coefficients

Table 4 Memory requirements and time for Ildefons' code

Script	Time (dd:hh:mm:ss)	Memory
makeMat.R	00:00:09:29	10.937 G
makeoo.m	00:04:22:15	09.617 G
makeFeatures.R	02:07:37:25 (normal-1)	30.051 G (normal-1)
	00:12:28:46 (normal-2)	22.287 G (normal-2)
	00:12:24:17 (valid)	23.046 G (valid)
	00:12:24:47 (test)	23.055 G (test)
normalizeFeatures.R	00:00:48:44	44.541 G
fitModels.R	00:02:05:38	12.339 G
createSolution.R	00:00:10:23	27.082 G

Table 5 Memory requirements and time for Lukasz's code

Seed	Max memory	Time (dd:hh:mm:ss)	AUC
1	31.566 G	02:23:47:32	0.93618
2	31.566 G	02:23:24:37	0.93663
3	31.566 G	03:00:18:40	0.93646
4	31.566 G	03:00:28:06	0.93614
5	31.566 G	02:23:50:08	0.93618
6	31.566 G	02:23:52:20	0.93564
7	31.566 G	02:23:51:33	0.93658
8	31.566 G	02:23:42:50	0.93579

- train and test a predictor based on such coefficients.

The Matlab sample code is suitable to get started. We provide a script (challengeFastBaseline) that computes a solution to the challenge (big "valid" and "test" datasets) in a few minutes, on a regular laptop computer. This uses Pearson's correlation coefficient (Correlation benchmark, AUC = 0.87322 on the public leaderboard). The data are first discretized with a simple method. Using more elaborate discretization methods such as OOPSI may work better. The other network reconstruction methods, including GTE, are not optimized: they are slow and requires a lot of memory.

C++: Network-reconstruction.org provides C++ code which would help participants to:

- read the data
- prepare a sample submission
- compute the GTE coefficient and a few other causal direction coefficients.

Note: The fluorescence matrices for small networks have dimension 179498×100 and of large networks 179500×1000. Even though the GTE code is "optimized" it is still slow and requires 10–12 h of computation for the big 1000 neuron networks on a compute cluster.

Python: We are providing scripts that:

- read the data
- discretizes
- prepare a sample submission using correlation.

One participant also made Python code available.

The baseline network reconstruction method, which we implemented, is described in details in (Stetter et al. 2012). It is based on Generalized Transfer Entropy (GTE), which is an extension of Transfer Entropy first introduced by Schreiber (Schreiber 2000), a measure that quantifies predictive information flow between stationary systems evolving in time. It is given by the Kulback–Leibler divergence between two models of a given time series, conditioned on a given dynamical state of the system, which in the case of fluorescence signals corresponds to the population average. Transfer Entropy captures linear and non-linear interactions between any pair of neurons in the network and is model-free, i.e. it does not require any a priori knowledge on the type of interaction between neurons. Apart from GTE, we have also provided the implementation of cross correlation and two information gain (IG) measures based on entropy and gini for network reconstruction. Cross correlation gives best results when there are zero time delays, which reduces it to a simple correlation coefficient measure. Hence, all these methods treat the data as independent instances/points in space instead of time series data. Another module that we have added to our software kit is a supervised learner, which extracts features from a network whose ground truth values are known and builds a simple linear classifier for learning whether a connection is present between two neurons or not. Currently, the features extracted are GTE, correlation, information gain using gini and information gain using entropy.

Appendix C. Description of the Algorithms of the Winners

We provide a high level description of the method of the top ranking participants provided in their fact sheets.

Team: AAAGV

The key point is building an undirected network through partial correlations, estimated through inverse covariance matrix. As preprocessing they use a combination of low and high pass filters to filter the signals and they try to filter out bursts or peak neural activities. They stress that their main contribution is the preprocessing of the data. The calcium fluorescence signal is generally very noisy due to light scattering artifacts. In the first step, a low pass filter is used to smooth the signal and filter out high frequency noise. To only retain high frequency around spikes, the time series is transformed into its backward difference. A hard-threshold filter is next applied to eliminate small variances and negative values. In a final step, another function is applied to magnify spikes that occur in cases of low global activity.

For inference, this team assumed that the fluorescence of the neurons at each point can be modeled as random variables independently drawn from the same time-invariant joint probability distribution. They then used partial correlation to detect direct associations between neurons and filter out spurious ones. Partial correlation measures contain dependence between variables and has been used for inference in gene regulatory networks De La Fuente et al. (2004); Schäfer and Strimmer (2005).

As the partial correlation matrix is symmetric, this method was not useful in detecting directionality. Some improvement was obtained by choosing an appropriate number of principal components. The method was sensitive to the choice of filter parameters.

Team: Matthias Ossadnik

He uses multivariate logistic regression of inferred spike trains (thresholded derivative signals). Then the scores of the regressive model are fed into a modified AdaBoost Freund and Schapire (1995) classifier together with other information, such as neuronal firing rates.

Team: Ildefons Magrans

Ildefons designed a feature engineering pipeline based on information about connectivity between neurons and optimized for a particular noise level and firing rate between neurons. Instead of using a single connectivity indicator, he optimizes several indicators. As a first step, he used OOPSI, which is based on the sequential Monte-Carlo methods, in his spike inference module. Spikes below a noise-level are treated as background noise and removed. After that, time steps containing spiking activity above the synchronization rate are removed as inter-bursts recordings are more informative for topology reconstruction. As connectivity indicator, he used plain correlation which however did not provide any directionality information. In order to eliminate arbitrary path lengths caused by direct and indirect effects, he used network deconvolution Feizi et al. (2013) which takes into account the entire connectivity matrix. The classifiers he uses with the features generated from correlation are Random Forests Liaw and Wiener (2002) and Gradient Boosting Machines Ridgeway (2006).

This method also could not identify directions of connections and correlation and the singular value decomposition step of network deconvolution had an extremely high computational complexity.

Team: Lukasz8000

Convolutional Neural Networks (CNN) go beyond feed forward neural networks in their ability to identify spatial dependencies and pattern recognition. CNNs recognize smaller patterns or feature maps in each layer eventually generalizing to more complex patterns in subsequent layers. Each convolutional layer is defined by the number and shapes of filters it has alongwith its ability to learn patterns. In addition, max pooling Boureau et al. (2010) is used to reduce the size of the generated feature maps.

He uses a deep convolutional neuronal network LeCun et al. (1998) to learn features of pairs of time-series hinting at the existence of a connection. In addition he also introduces an additional input layer, the average activity of network. Lukasz used preprocessing to retain regions of higher activity conditioned on a particular threshold. These active regions help to detect interdependencies. The other important choice which influenced results was that of an activation function. He used tanh in the first convolutional layer followed by Rectified Linear Unit Nair and Hinton (2010) in the next two layers. To improve the network structure, he used max pooling. Gradient descent was combined with momentum Polyak (1964) and this helped to navigate past local extrema.

References

Lionel Barnett, Adam B Barrett, and Anil K Seth. Granger causality and transfer entropy are equivalent for gaussian variables. *Physical review letters*, 103(23):238701, 2009.

P Bonifazi, M Goldin, M A Picardo, I Jorquera, A Cattani, G Bianconi, a Represa, Y Ben-Ari, and R Cossart. GABAergic hub neurons orchestrate synchrony in developing hippocampal networks. *Science (New York, N.Y.)*, 326(5958):1419–24, December 2009. ISSN 1095-9203.

Y-Lan Boureau, Jean Ponce, and Yann LeCun. A theoretical analysis of feature pooling in visual recognition. In *Proceedings of the 27th International Conference on Machine Learning (ICML-10)*, pages 111–118, 2010.

Andrew P Bradley. The use of the area under the roc curve in the evaluation of machine learning algorithms. *Pattern recognition*, 30(7):1145–1159, 1997.

Leo Breiman. Random forests. *Machine learning*, 45(1):5–32, 2001.

Wojciech M. Czarnecki and Rafal Jozefowicz. Neural connectivity reconstruction from calcium imaging signal using random forest with topological features. *JMLR, proceedings track*, This volume, 2014.

Ildefons Magrans de Abril and Ann Nowe. Supervised neural network structure recovery. *JMLR, proceedings track*, This volume, 2014.

Alberto De La Fuente, Nan Bing, Ina Hoeschele, and Pedro Mendes. Discovery of meaningful associations in genomic data using partial correlation coefficients. *Bioinformatics*, 20(18):3565–3574, 2004.

J Eckmann, O Feinerman, L Gruendlinger, E Moses, J Soriano, and T Tlusty. The physics of living neural networks. *Physics Reports*, 449(1-3):54–76, September 2007. ISSN 03701573.

Soheil Feizi, Daniel Marbach, Muriel Médard, and Manolis Kellis. Network deconvolution as a general method to distinguish direct dependencies in networks. *Nature biotechnology*, 2013.

Yoav Freund and Robert E Schapire. A desicion-theoretic generalization of on-line learning and an application to boosting. In *Computational learning theory*, pages 23–37. Springer, 1995.

Marc-Oliver Gewaltig and Markus Diesmann. Nest (neural simulation tool). *Scholarpedia*, 2(4):1430, 2007.

Benjamin F Grewe, Dominik Langer, Hansjörg Kasper, Björn M Kampa, and Fritjof Helmchen. High-speed in vivo calcium imaging reveals neuronal network activity with near-millisecond precision. *Nature methods*, 7(5):399–405, May 2010. ISSN 1548-7105.

Christine Grienberger and Arthur Konnerth. Imaging calcium in neurons. *Neuron*, 73(5):862–885, 2012.

Sten Grillner. Megascience efforts and the brain. *Neuron*, 82(6):1209–11, June 2014. ISSN 1097-4199.

Isabelle Guyon, Demian Battaglia, Alice Guyon, Vincent Lemaire, Javier G Orlandi, Mehreen Saeed, Jordi Soriano, Alexander Statnikov, Olav Stetter, and Bisakha Ray. Design of the first neuronal connectomics challenge: From imaging to connectivity. *Neural Networks (IJCNN), 2014 International Joint Conference on*, pages 2600–2607, July 2014.

Eric R Kandel, Henry Markram, Paul M Matthews, Rafael Yuste, and Christof Koch. Neuroscience thinks big (and collaboratively). *Nature reviews. Neuroscience*, 14(9):659–64, September 2013.

Yann LeCun, Léon Bottou, Yoshua Bengio, and Patrick Haffner. Gradient-based learning applied to document recognition. *Proceedings of the IEEE*, 86(11):2278–2324, 1998.

Andy Liaw and Matthew Wiener. Classification and regression by randomforest. *R news*, 2(3):18–22, 2002.

Vinod Nair and Geoffrey E Hinton. Rectified linear units improve restricted boltzmann machines. In *Proceedings of the 27th International Conference on Machine Learning (ICML-10)*, pages 807–814, 2010.

Kenichi Ohki, Sooyoung Chung, Yeang H Ch'ng, Prakash Kara, and R Clay Reid. Functional imaging with cellular resolution reveals precise micro-architecture in visual cortex. *Nature*, 433(7026):597–603, February 2005. ISSN 1476-4687.

Javier G. Orlandi, Jordi Soriano, Enrique Alvarez-Lacalle, Sara Teller, and Jaume Casademunt. Noise focusing and the emergence of coherent activity in neuronal cultures. *Nature Physics*, 9(9):582–590, 2013.

Javier G Orlandi, Olav Stetter, Jordi Soriano, Theo Geisel, and Demian Battaglia. Transfer entropy reconstruction and labeling of neuronal connections from simulated calcium imaging. *PLoS One*, 9(6):e98842, 2014.

Thomas Panier, Sebastián a Romano, Raphaël Olive, Thomas Pietri, Germán Sumbre, Raphaël Candelier, and Georges Debrégeas. Fast functional imaging of multiple brain regions in intact zebrafish larvae using Selective Plane Illumination Microscopy. *Frontiers in neural circuits*, 7(April):65, January 2013. ISSN 1662-5110.

Boris Teodorovich Polyak. Some methods of speeding up the convergence of iteration methods. *USSR Computational Mathematics and Mathematical Physics*, 4(5):1–17, 1964.

Greg Ridgeway. Generalized boosted regression models. *Documentation on the R Package gbm, version 1· 5*, 7, 2006.

Lukasz Romaszko. Signal correlation prediction using convolutional neural networks. *JMLR, proceedings track*, This volume, 2014.

Srikanth Ryali, Tianwen Chen, Kaustubh Supekar, and Vinod Menon. Estimation of functional connectivity in fmri data using stability selection-based sparse partial correlation with elastic net penalty. *Neuroimage*, 59(4):3852–3861, 2012.

Juliane Schäfer and Korbinian Strimmer. A shrinkage approach to large-scale covariance matrix estimation and implications for functional genomics. *Statistical applications in genetics and molecular biology*, 4(1), 2005.

Thomas Schreiber. Measuring information transfer. *Physical review letters*, 85(2):461, 2000.

Micha E Spira and Aviad Hai. Multi-electrode array technologies for neuroscience and cardiology. *Nature nanotechnology*, 8(2):83–94, February 2013. ISSN 1748-3395.

Olav Stetter, Demian Battaglia, Jordi Soriano, and Theo Geisel. Model-free reconstruction of excitatory neuronal connectivity from calcium imaging signals. *PLoS computational biology*, 8(8):e1002653, 2012.

Antonio Sutera, Arnaud Joly, Vincent Francois-Lavet, Zixiao Aaron Qiu, Gilles Louppe, Damien Ernst, and Pierre Geurts. Simple connectome inference from partial correlation statistics in calcium imaging. *JMLR, proceedings track*, This volume, 2014.

Chenyang Tao, Wei Lin, and Jianfeng Feng. Reconstruction of excitatory neuronal connectivity via metric score pooling and regularization. *JMLR, proceedings track*, This volume, 2014.

Elisenda Tibau, Miguel Valencia, and Jordi Soriano. Identification of neuronal network properties from the spectral analysis of calcium imaging signals in neuronal cultures. *Frontiers in neural circuits*, 7(December):199, January 2013. ISSN 1662-5110.

Joshua T Vogelstein. *OOPSI: A family of optimal optical spike inference algorithms for inferring neural connectivity from population calcium imaging*. THE JOHNS HOPKINS UNIVERSITY, 2009.

Joshua T Vogelstein, Brendon O Watson, Adam M Packer, Rafael Yuste, Bruno Jedynak, and Liam Paninski. Spike inference from calcium imaging using sequential monte carlo methods. *Biophysical journal*, 97(2):636–655, 2009.

Duncan J. Watts and Steven H. Strogatz. Collective dynamics of 'small-world' networks. *Nature*, 393(6684):440–442, June 1998.

Jason Weston, Frédéric Ratle, Hossein Mobahi, and Ronan Collobert. Deep learning via semi-supervised embedding. In *Neural Networks: Tricks of the Trade*, pages 639–655. Springer, 2012.

BC Wheeler and GJ Brewer. Designing neural networks in culture. *Proceedings of the IEEE*, 98(3), 2010.

Rafael Yuste and George M. Church. The New Century of the Brain. *Scientific American*, 310(3):38–45, February 2014.

Simple Connectome Inference from Partial Correlation Statistics in Calcium Imaging

Antonio Sutera, Arnaud Joly, Vincent Franois-Lavet,
Zixiao Aaron Qiu, Gilles Louppe, Damien Ernst and Pierre Geurts

Editors: Demian Battaglia, Isabelle Guyon, Vincent Lemaire,
Javier Orlandi, Bisakha Ray, Jordi Soriano

Abstract In this work, we propose a simple yet effective solution to the problem of connectome inference in calcium imaging data. The proposed algorithm consists of two steps. First, processing the raw signals to detect neural peak activities. Second, inferring the degree of association between neurons from partial correlation statistics. This paper summarises the methodology that led us to win the Connectomics Challenge, proposes a simplified version of our method, and finally compares our results with respect to other inference methods.

Keywords Connectomics · Network inference · Partial correlation

1 Introduction

The human brain is a complex biological organ made of about 100 billion of neurons, each connected to, on average, 7,000 other neurons (Pakkenberg et al. 2003). Unfortunately, direct observation of the connectome, the wiring diagram of the brain, is not yet technically feasible. Without being perfect, calcium imaging currently allows for real-time and simultaneous observation of neuron activity from thousands of neurons, producing individual time-series representing their fluorescence intensity. From

The original form of this article appears in JMLR W&CP Volume 46.

A. Sutera (✉) · A. Joly · V. Franois-Lavet · Z. Aaron Qiu · G. Louppe ·
D. Ernst · P. Geurts
Department of EE and CS & GIGA-R, University of Liège, Liège, Belgium
e-mail: a.sutera@ulg.ac.be

© Springer International Publishing AG 2017

D. Battaglia et al. (eds.), *Neural Connectomics Challenge*, The Springer Series
on Challenges in Machine Learning, DOI 10.1007/978-3-319-53070-3_2

23

these data, the connectome inference problem amounts to retrieving the synaptic connections between neurons on the basis of the fluorescence time-series. This problem is difficult to solve because of experimental issues, including masking effects (i.e. some of the neurons are not observed or confounded with others), the low sampling rate of the optical device with respect to the neural activity speed, or the slow decay of fluorescence.

Formally, the connectome can be represented as a directed graph $G = (V, E)$, where V is a set of p nodes representing neurons, and $E \subseteq \{(i, j) \in V \times V\}$ is a set of edges representing direct synaptic connections between neurons. Causal interactions are expressed by the direction of edges: $(i, j) \in E$ indicates that the state of neuron j might be caused by the activity of neuron i. In those terms, the connectome inference problem is formally stated as follows: *Given the sampled observations $\{x_i^t \in \mathbb{R} | i \in V, t = 1, \ldots, T\}$ of p neurons for T time intervals, the goal is to infer the set E of connections in G.*

In this paper, we present a simplified - and almost as good - version of the winning method[1] of the Connectomics Challenge,[2] as a simple and theoretically grounded approach based on signal processing techniques and partial correlation statistics. The paper is structured as follows: Sect. 2 describes the signal processing methods applied on fluorescent calcium time-series; Sect. 3 then presents the proposed approach and its theoretical properties; Sect. 4 provides an empirical analysis and comparison with other network inference methods, while finally, in Sect. 5 we discuss our work and provide further research directions. Additionally, Appendix A further describes, in full detail, our actual winning method which gives slightly better results than the method presented in this paper, at the cost of parameter tuning. Appendix B provides supplementary results on other datasets.

2 Signal Processing

Under the simplifying assumption that neurons are on-off units, characterised by short periods of intense activity, or peaks, and longer periods of inactivity, the first part of our algorithm consists of cleaning the raw fluorescence data. More specifically, time-series are processed using standard signal processing filters in order to: (i) remove noise mainly due to fluctuations independent of calcium, calcium fluctuations independent of spiking activity, calcium fluctuations in nearby tissues that have been mistakenly captured, or simply by the imaging process; (ii) to account for fluorescence low decay; and (iii) to reduce the importance of high global activity in the network. The overall process is illustrated in Fig. 1.

As Fig. 1a shows, the raw fluorescence signal is very noisy due to light scattering artifacts that usually affect the quality of the recording (Lichtman and Denk 2011). Accordingly, the first step of our pipeline is to smoothe the signal, using one of the

---

[1]Code available at https://github.com/asutera/kaggle-connectomics.

[2]http://connectomics.chalearn.org.

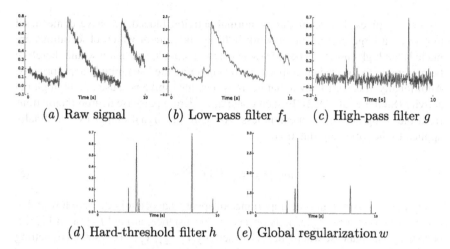

(a) Raw signal (b) Low-pass filter f_1 (c) High-pass filter g

(d) Hard-threshold filter h (e) Global regularization w

Fig. 1 Signal processing pipeline for extracting peaks from the raw fluorescence data

following low-pass filters for filtering out high frequency noise:

$$f_1(x_i^t) = x_i^{t-1} + x_i^t + x_i^{t+1}, \tag{1}$$
$$f_2(x_i^t) = 0.4x_i^{t-3} + 0.6x_i^{t-2} + 0.8x_i^{t-1} + x_i^t. \tag{2}$$

These filters are standard in the signal processing field (Kaiser and Reed 1977; Oppenheim et al. 1983). For the purposes of illustration, the effect of the filter f_1 on the signal is shown in Fig. 1b.

Furthermore, short spikes, characterized by a high frequency, can be seen as an indirect indicator of neuron communication, while low frequencies of the signal mainly correspond to the slow decay of fluorescence. To have a signal that only has high magnitude around instances where the spikes occur, the second step of our pipeline transforms the time-series into its backward difference

$$g(x_i^t) = x_i^t - x_i^{t-1}, \tag{3}$$

as shown in Fig. 1c.

To filter out small variations in the signal obtained after applying the function g, as well as to eliminate negative values, we use the following hard-threshold filter

$$h(x_i^t) = x_i^t \mathbb{1}(x_i^t \geq \tau) \text{ with } \tau > 0, \tag{4}$$

yielding Fig. 1d where τ is the threshold parameter and $\mathbb{1}$ is the indicator function. As can be seen, the processed signal only contains clean spikes.

The objective of the last step of our filtering procedure is to decrease the importance of spikes that occur when there is high global activity in the network with respect to spikes that occur during normal activity. Indeed, we have conjectured that when a large part of the network is firing, the rate at which observations are made is not high enough to be able to detect interactions, and that it would therefore be preferable to lower their importance by changing their magnitude appropriately. Additionally, it is well-known that neurons may also spike because of a high global activity (Stetter et al. 2012). In such context, detecting pairwise neuron interactions from the firing activity is meaningless. As such, the signal output by h is finally applied to the following function

$$w(x_i^t) = (x_i^t + 1)^{1 + \frac{1}{\sum_j x_j^t}}, \tag{5}$$

whose effect is to magnify the importance of spikes that occur in cases of low global activity (measured by $\sum_j x_j^t$), as observed, for instance, around $t = 4s$ in Fig. 1e. Note the particular case where there is no activity, i.e. $\sum_j x_j^t = 0$, is solved by setting $w(x_i^t) = 1$.

To summarise, the full signal processing pipeline of our simplified approach is defined by the composed function $w \circ h \circ g \circ f_1$ (resp. f_2). When applied to the raw signal of Fig. 1a, it outputs the signal shown in Fig. 1e.

3 Connectome Inference from Partial Correlation Statistics

Our procedure to infer connections between neurons first assumes that the (filtered) fluorescence concentrations of all p neurons at each time point can be modelled as a set of random variables $X = \{X_1, \ldots, X_p\}$ that are independently drawn from the same time-invariant joint probability distribution P_X. As a consequence, our inference method does not exploit the time-ordering of the observations (although time-ordering is exploited by the filters).

Given this assumption, we then propose to use as a measure of the strength of the connection between two neurons i and j, the *Partial correlation* coefficient $p_{i,j}$ between their corresponding random variables X_i and X_j, defined by:

$$p_{i,j} = -\frac{\Sigma_{ij}^{-1}}{\sqrt{\Sigma_{ii}^{-1} \Sigma_{jj}^{-1}}}, \tag{6}$$

where Σ^{-1}, known as the precision or concentration matrix, is the inverse of the covariance matrix Σ of X. Assuming that the distribution P_X is a multivariate Gaussian distribution $\mathcal{N}(\mu, \Sigma)$, it can be shown that $p_{i,j}$ is zero if and only if X_i and X_j are independent given all other variables in X, i.e. $X_i \perp X_j | X^{-i,j}$ where $X^{-i,j} = X \setminus \{X_i, X_j\}$. Partial correlation thus measures conditional dependencies between variables; therefore it should naturally only detect direct associations between neurons and filter out spurious indirect effects. The interest of partial correlation as an association measure has already been shown for the inference of gene regulatory networks (De La Fuente et al. 2004; Schäfer and Strimmer 2005). Note that the partial correlation statistic is symmetric (i.e. $p_{i,j} = p_{j,i}$). Therefore, our approach cannot identify the direction of the interactions between neurons. We will see in Sect. 4 why this only slightly affects its performance, with respect to the metric used in the Connectomics Challenge.

Practically speaking, the computation of all $p_{i,j}$ coefficients using Eq. 6 requires the estimation of the covariance matrix Σ and then computing its inverse. Given that typically we have more samples than neurons, the covariance matrix can be inverted in a straightforward way. We nevertheless obtained some improvement by replacing the exact inverse with an approximation using only the M first principal components (Bishop 2006) (with $M = 0.8p$ in our experiments, see Appendix C).

Finally, it should be noted that the performance of our simple method appears to be quite sensitive to the values of parameters (e.g. choice of f_1 or f_2 or the value of the threshold τ) in the combined function of the filtering and inferring processes. One approach, further referred to as *Averaged Partial correlation* statistics, for improving its robustness is to average correlation statistics over various values of the parameters, thereby reducing the variance of its predictions. Further details about parameter selection are provided in Appendix A.

4 Experiments

Data and evaluation metrics. We report here experiments on the *normal –1, 2, 3,* and *4* datasets provided by the organisers of the Connectomics Challenge (see Appendix B for experiments on other datasets). Each of these datasets is obtained from the simulation (Stetter et al. 2012) of different neural networks of 1,000 neurons and approximately 15,000 edges (i.e. a network density of about 1.5%). Each neuron is described by a calcium fluorescence time-series of length $T = 179500$. All inference methods compared here provide a ranking of all pairs of neurons according to some association score. To assess the quality of this ranking, we compute both ROC and precision-recall curves against the ground-truth network, which are represented by the area under the curves and respectively denoted AUROC and AUPRC. Only the AUROC score was used to rank the challenge participants, but the precision-recall curve has been shown to be a more sensible metric for network inference, especially when network density is small (see e.g. Schrynemackers et al. 2013). Since neurons are not self-connected in the ground-truth networks (i.e. $(i, i) \notin E, \forall i \in V$), we have manually set the score of such edges to the minimum possible association score before computing ROC and PR curves.

Evaluation of the method. The top of Table 1 reports AUROC and AUPRC for all four networks using, in each case, partial correlation with different filtering functions. Except for the last two rows that use PCA, the exact inverse of the covariance matrix was used in each case. These results clearly show the importance of the filters.

Table 1 Top: Performance on *normal −1, 2, 3, 4* with partial correlation and different filtering functions. Bottom: Performance on *normal −1, 2, 3, 4* with different methods

Method \ normal-	AUROC				AUPRC			
	1	2	3	4	1	2	3	4
No filtering	0.777	0.767	0.772	0.774	0.070	0.064	0.068	0.072
$h \circ g \circ f_1$	0.923	0.925	0.923	0.922	0.311	0.315	0.313	0.304
$w \circ h \circ g \circ f_1$	0.931	0.929	0.928	0.926	0.326	0.323	0.319	0.303
+ PCA	0.932	0.930	0.928	0.926	0.355	0.353	0.350	0.333
Averaging	0.937	0.935	0.935	0.931	0.391	0.390	0.385	0.375
Full method	**0.943**	**0.942**	**0.942**	**0.939**	**0.403**	**0.404**	**0.398**	**0.388**
PC	0.886	0.884	0.891	0.877	0.153	0.145	0.170	0.132
GTE	0.890	0.893	0.894	0.873	0.171	0.174	0.197	0.142
GENIE3	0.892	0.891	0.887	0.887	0.232	0.221	0.237	0.215

AUROC increases in average from 0.77 to 0.93. PCA does not really affect AUROC scores, but it significantly improves AUPRC scores. Taking the average over various parameter settings gives an improvement of 10% in AUPRC but only a minor change in AUROC. The last row ("Full method") shows the final performance of the method specifically tuned for the challenge (see Appendix A for all details). Although this tuning was decisive to obtain the best performance in the challenge, it does not significantly improve either AUROC or AUPRC.

Comparison with other methods. At the bottom of Table 1, we provide as a comparison the performance of three other methods: standard (Pearson) correlation (PC), generalised transfer entropy (GTE), and GENIE3. ROC and PR curves on the *normal-2* network are shown for all methods in Fig. 2. Pearson correlation measures the unconditional linear (in)dependence between variables and it should thus not be able to filter out indirect interactions between neurons. GTE (Stetter et al. 2012) was proposed as a baseline for the challenge. This method builds on Transfer Entropy to measure the association between two neurons. Unlike our approach, it can predict the direction of the edges. GENIE3 (Huynh-Thu et al. 2010) is a gene regulatory network inference method that was the best performer in the DREAM5 challenge (Marbach et al. 2012). When transposed to neural networks, this method uses the importance score of variable X_i in a Random Forest model trying to predict X_j from all variables in $X \setminus X_j$ as a confidence score for the edge going from neuron i to neuron j. However, to reduce the computational cost of this method, we had to limit each tree in the Random Forest model to a maximum depth of 3. This constraint has a potentially severe effect on the performance of this method with respect to the use of fully-grown trees. PC and GENIE3 were applied to the time-series filtered using the functions $w \circ h \circ g$ and $h \circ g \circ f_1$ (which gave the best performance), respectively. For GENIE3, we built 10,000 trees per neuron and we used default settings for all other parameters (except for the maximal tree depth). For GTE, we reproduced

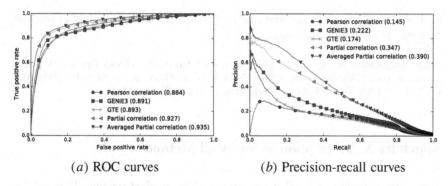

(*a*) ROC curves   (*b*) Precision-recall curves

Fig. 2 ROC (*left*) and PR (*right*) curves on *normal-2* for the compared methods. Areas under the curves are reported in the legend

the exact same setting (conditioning level and pre-processing) that was used by the organisers of the challenge.

Partial correlation and averaged partial correlation clearly outperform all other methods on all datasets (see Table 1 and Appendix B). The improvement is more important in terms of AUPRC than in terms of AUROC. As expected, Pearson correlation performs very poorly in terms of AUPRC. GTE and GENIE3 work much better, but these two methods are nevertheless clearly below partial correlation. Among these two methods, GTE is slightly better in terms of AUROC, while GENIE3 is significantly better in terms of AUPRC. Given that we had to limit this latter method for computational reasons, these results are very promising and a comparison with the full GENIE3 approach is certainly part of our future works.

The fact that our method is unable to predict edge directions does not seem to be a disadvantage with respect to GTE and GENIE3. Although partial correlation scores each edge, and its opposite, similarly, it can reach precision values higher than 0.5 (see Fig. 2b), suggesting that it mainly ranks high pairs of neurons that interact in both directions. It is interesting also to note that, on *normal-2*, a method that perfectly predicts the undirected network (i.e. that gives a score of 1 to each pair (i, j) such that $(i, j) \in E$ or $(j, i) \in E$, and 0 otherwise) already reaches an AUROC as high as 0.995 and an AUPRC of 0.789.

5 Conclusions

In this paper, we outlined a simple but efficient methodology for the problem of connectome inference from calcium imaging data. Our approach consists of two steps: (i) processing fluorescence data to detect neural peak activities; and (ii) inferring the degree of association between neurons from partial correlation statistics. Its simplified variant outperforms other network inference methods while its optimized version proved to be the best method on the Connectomics Challenge. Given its simplicity and good performance, we therefore believe that the methodology presented in this work would constitute a solid and easily-reproducible baseline for further work in the field of connectome inference.

Acknowledgements A. Joly and G. Louppe are research fellows of the FNRS, Belgium. A. Sutera is a recipient of an FRIA fellowship of FRS-FNRS, Belgium. This work is supported by PASCAL2 and the IUAP DYSCO, initiated by the Belgian State, Science Policy Office.

Appendix A. Description of the "Full Method"

This section provides a detailed description of the method specifically tuned for the Connectomics Challenge. We restrict our description to the differences with respect to the simplified method presented in the main paper. Most parameters were tuned so as to maximize AUROC on the *normal-1* dataset and our design choices were validated by monitoring the AUROC obtained by the 145 entries we submitted during the challenge. Although the tuned method performs better than the simplified one on the challenge dataset, we believe that the tuned method clearly overfits the simulator used to generate the challenge data and that the simplified method should work equally well on new independent datasets. We nevertheless provide the tuned method here for reference purposes. Our implementation of the tuned method is available at https://github.com/asutera/kaggle-connectomics.

This appendix is structured as follows: Sect. A.1 describes the differences in terms of signal processing. Section A.2 then provides a detailed presentation of the averaging approach. Section A.3 presents an approach to correct the $p_{i,j}$ values so as to take into account the edge directionality. Finally, Sect. A.4 presents some experimental results to validate the different steps of our proposal.

A.1 Signal Processing

In Sect. 2, we introduced four filtering functions (f, g, h, and w) that are composed in sequence (i.e. $w \circ h \circ g \circ f$) to provide the signals from which to compute partial correlation statistics. Filtering is modified as follows in the tuned method:

- In addition to f_1 and f_2 (Eqs. 1 and 2), two alternative low-pass filters f_3 and f_4 are considered:

$$f_3(x_i^t) = x_i^{t-1} + x_i^t + x_i^{t+1} + x_i^{t+2}, \qquad (7)$$

$$f_4(x_i^t) = x_i^t + x_i^{t+1} + x_i^{t+2} + x_i^{t+3}. \qquad (8)$$

- An additional filter r is applied to smoothe differences in peak magnitudes that might remain after the application of the hard-threshold filter h:

$$r(x_i^t) = (x_i^t)^c, \tag{9}$$

with $c = 0.9$.

- Filter w is replaced by a more complex filter w^* defined as:

$$w^*(x_i^t) = (x_i^t + 1)^{\left(1 + \frac{1}{\sum_j x_j^t}\right)^{k\left(\sum_j x_j^t\right)}}, \tag{10}$$

where the function k is a piecewise linear function optimised separately for each filter f_1, f_2, f_3 and f_4 (see the implementation for full details). Filter w in the simplified method is a special case of w^* with $k(\sum_j x_j^t) = 1$.

The pre-processed time-series are then obtained by the application of the following function: $w^* \circ r \circ h \circ g \circ f_i$ (with $i = 1, 2, 3,$ or 4).

A.2 Weighted Average of Partial Correlation Statistics

As discussed in Sect. 3, the performance of the method (in terms of AUROC) is sensitive to the value of the parameter τ of the hard-threshold filter h (see Eq. 4), and to the choice of the low-pass filter (among $\{f_1, f_2, f_3, f_4\}$). As in the simplified method, we have averaged the partial correlation statistics obtained for all the pairs $(\tau,$ low-pass filter$) \in \{0.100, 0.101, \ldots, 0.209\} \times \{f_1, f_2, f_3, f_4\}$.

Filters f_1 and f_2 display similar performances and thus were given similar weights (i.e. resp. 0.383 and 0.345). These weights were chosen equal to the weights selected for the simplified method. In contrast, filters f_3 and f_4 turn out, individually, to be less competitive and were therefore given less importance in the weighted average (i.e. resp. 0.004 and 0.268). Yet, as further shown in Sect. A.4, combining all 4 filters proves to marginally improve performance with respect to using only f_1 and f_2.

A.3 Prediction of Edge Orientation

Partial correlation statistics is a symmetric measure, while the connectome is a directed graph. It could thus be beneficial to try to predict edge orientation. In this section, we present an heuristic that modifies the p_{ij} computed by the approach described before which takes into account directionality.

This approach is based on the following observation. The rise of fluorescence of a neuron indicates its activation. If another neuron is activated after a slight delay, this could be a consequence of the activation of the first neuron and therefore indicates a directed link in the connectome from the first to the second neuron. Given this observation, we have computed the following term for every pair (i, j):

$$s_{i,j} = \sum_{t=1}^{T-1} \mathbb{1}((x_j^{t+1} - x_i^t) \in [\phi_1, \phi_2]), \tag{11}$$

that could be interpreted as an image of the number of times that neuron i activates neuron j. ϕ_1 and ϕ_2 are parameters whose values have been chosen in our experiments equal to 0.2 and 0.5, respectively. Their role is to define when the difference between x_j^{t+1} and x_i^t can indeed be assimilated to an event for which neuron i activates neuron j.

Afterwards, we have computed the difference between $s_{i,j}$ and $s_{j,i}$, that we call $z_{i,j}$, and used this difference to modify $p_{i,j}$ and $p_{j,i}$ so as to take into account directionality. Naturally, if $z_{i,j}$ is greater (smaller) than 0, we may conclude that should there be an edge between i and j, then this edge would have to be oriented from i to j (j to i).

This suggests the new association matrix r:

$$r_{i,j} = \mathbb{1}(z_{i,j} > \phi_3) * p_{i,j} \tag{12}$$

where $\phi_3 > 0$ is another parameter. We discovered that this new matrix r was not providing good results, probably due to the fact that directivity was not rewarded well enough in the challenge.

This has lead us to investigate other ways for exploiting the information about directionality contained in the matrix z. One of those ways that gave good performance was to use as an association matrix:

$$q_{i,j} = weight * p_{i,j} + (1 - weight) * z_{i,j} \tag{13}$$

with $weight$ chosen close to 1 ($weight = 0.997$). Note that with values for $weight$ close to 1, matrix q only uses the information to a minimum about directivity contained in z to modify the partial correlation matrix p. We tried smaller values for $weight$ but those provided poorer results.

It was this association matrix $q_{i,j}$ that actually led to the best results of the challenge, as shown in Table 3 of Sect. A.4.

A.4 Experiments

On the interest of low-pass filters f_3 and f_4. As reported in Table 2, averaging over all low-pass filters leads to better AUROC scores than averaging over only two low-pass filters, i.e. f_1 and f_2. However this slightly reduces AUPRC.

On the interest of using matrix q rather than p to take into account directivity. Table 3 compares AUROC and AUPRC with or without correcting the $p_{i,j}$ values according to Eq. 13. Both AUROC and AUPRC are (very slightly) improved by using information about directivity.

Appendix B. Supplementary Results

In this appendix we report the performance of the different methods compared in the paper on 6 additional datasets provided by the Challenge organisers. These datasets, corresponding each to networks of 1,000 neurons, are similar to the *normal* datasets except for one feature:

lowcon: Similar network but on average with a lower number of connections per neuron.

highcon: Similar network but on average with a higher number of connections per neuron.

lowcc: Similar network but on average with a lower clustering coefficient.

highcc: Similar network but on average with a higher clustering coefficient.

normal-3-highrate: Same topology as *normal-3* but with a higher firing frequency, i.e. with highly active neurons.

normal-4-lownoise: Same topology as *normal-4* but with a better signal-to-noise ratio.

The results of several methods applied to these 6 datasets are provided in Table 4. They confirm what we observed on the *normal* datasets. Average partial correlation and its tuned variant, i.e. "Full method", clearly outperform other network inference methods on all datasets. PC is close to GENIE3 and GTE, but still slightly worse. GENIE3 performs better than GTE most of the time. Note that the"Full method" reported in this table does not use Eq. 13 to slightly correct the values of $p_{i,j}$ to take into account directivity.

Table 2 Performance on *normal −1, 2, 3,* or *4* with partial correlation with different averaging approaches

Averaging \ normal-	AUROC				AUPRC			
	1	*2*	*3*	*4*	*1*	*2*	*3*	*4*
with f_1, f_2	0.937	0.935	0.935	0.931	0.391	**0.390**	0.385	**0.375**
with f_1, f_2, f_3, f_4	**0.938**	**0.936**	**0.936**	**0.932**	0.391	0.389	0.385	0.374

Table 3 Performance on *normal −1, 2, 3, 4* of "Full Method" with and without using information about directivity

Full method \ normal-	AUROC				AUPRC			
	1	*2*	*3*	*4*	*1*	*2*	*3*	*4*
Undirected	0.943	0.942	0.942	0.939	0.403	0.404	0.398	0.388
Directed	**0.944**	**0.943**	0.942	**0.940**	**0.404**	**0.405**	**0.399**	**0.389**

Table 4 Performance (top: AUROC, bottom: AUPRC) on specific datasets with different methods

Method \ normal-	AUROC					
	lowcon	highcon	lowcc	highcc	3-highrate	4-lownoise
Averaging	0.947	0.943	0.920	0.942	0.959	0.934
Full method	**0.955**	**0.944**	**0.925**	**0.946**	**0.961**	**0.941**
PC	0.782	0.920	0.846	0.897	0.898	0.873
GTE	0.846	0.905	0.848	0.899	0.905	0.879
GENIE3	0.781	0.924	0.879	0.902	0.886	0.890
	AUPRC					
Averaging	0.320	0.429	0.262	0.478	0.443	0.412
Full method	**0.334**	**0.413**	**0.260**	**0.486**	**0.452**	**0.432**
PC	0.074	0.218	0.082	0.165	0.193	0.135
GTE	0.094	0.211	0.081	0.165	0.210	0.144
GENIE3	0.128	0.273	0.116	0.309	0.256	0.224

Appendix C. On the Selection of the Number of Principal Components

The (true) network, seen as a matrix, can be decomposed through a singular value decomposition (SVD) or principal component analysis (PCA), so as to respectively determine a set of independent linear combinations of the variable (Alter et al. 2000), or a reduced set of linear combinations combine, which then maximize the explained variance of the data (Jolliffe 2005). Since SVD and PCA are related, they can be defined by the same goal: both aim at finding a reduced set of neurons, known as components, whose activity can explain the rest of the network.

The distribution of component eigen values obtained from PCA and SVD decompositions can be studied by sorting them in descending order of magnitude, as illustrated in Fig. 3. It can be seen that some component eigen values are zero, implying that the behaviour of the network could be explained by a subset of neurons because of the redundancy and relations between the neurons. For all datasets, the eigen value distribution is exactly the same.

In the context of the challenge, we observe that only 800 components seem to be necessary and we exploit this when computing partial correlation statistics. Therefore, the value of the parameter M is immediate and should be clearly set to 800 ($=0.8p$).

Note that if the true network is not available, similar decomposition analysis could be carried on the inferred network, or on the data directly.

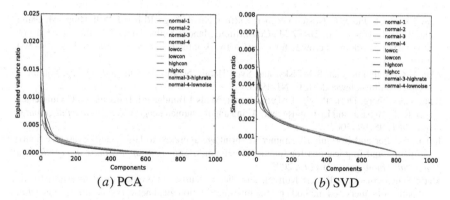

(a) PCA   (b) SVD

Fig. 3 Explained variance ratio by number of principal components (*left*) and singular value ratio by number of principal components (*right*) for all networks

Table 5 Connectomics challenge summary

Team name	The AAAGV team
Private leaderboard position	1st
Private leaderboard performance	0.94161
Private leaderboard performance of the winner	idem

Appendix D. Summary Table

See Table 5.

References

Orly Alter, Patrick O Brown, and David Botstein. Singular value decomposition for genome-wide expression data processing and modeling. *Proceedings of the National Academy of Sciences*, 97(18):10101–10106, 2000.

Christopher M Bishop. *Pattern recognition and machine learning*, volume 1. Springer New York, 2006.

Alberto De La Fuente, Nan Bing, Ina Hoeschele, and Pedro Mendes. Discovery of meaningful associations in genomic data using partial correlation coefficients. *Bioinformatics*, 20(18):3565–3574, 2004.

Vn Anh Huynh-Thu, Alexandre Irrthum, Louis Wehenkel, and Pierre Geurts. Inferring regulatory networks from expression data using tree-based methods. *PloS one*, 5(9):e12776, 2010.

Ian Jolliffe. *Principal component analysis*. Wiley Online Library, 2005.

JF Kaiser and WA Reed. Data smoothing using low-pass digital filters. *Review of Scientific Instruments*, 48(11):1447–1457, 1977.

Jeff W Lichtman and Winfried Denk. The big and the small: challenges of imaging the brains circuits. *Science*, 334(6056):618–623, 2011.

Daniel Marbach, James C. Costello, Robert Küffner, Nicole Vega, Robert J. Prill, Diogo M. Camacho, Kyle R. Allison, The DREAM5 Consortium, Manolis Kellis, James J. Collins, and Gustavo
Stolovitzky. Wisdom of crowds for robust network inference. *Nature methods*, 9(8):794–804,
2012.

Alan V Oppenheim, Alan S Willsky, and Syed Hamid Nawab. *Signals and systems*, volume 2.
Prentice-Hall Englewood Cliffs, NJ, 1983.

Bente Pakkenberg, Dorte Pelvig, Lisbeth Marner, Mads J Bundgaard, Hans Jørgen G Gundersen,
Jens R Nyengaard, and Lisbeth Regeur. Aging and the human neocortex. *Experimental gerontol-
ogy*, 38(1):95–99, 2003.

Juliane Schäfer and Korbinian Strimmer. A shrinkage approach to large-scale covariance matrix
estimation and implications for functional genomics. *Statistical applications in genetics and
molecular biology*, 4(32):1175, 2005.

Marie Schrynemackers, Robert Küffner, and Pierre Geurts. On protocols and measures for the
validation of supervised methods for the inference of biological networks. *Frontiers in genetics*,
4, 2013.

Olav Stetter, Demian Battaglia, Jordi Soriano, and Theo Geisel. Model-free reconstruction of
excitatory neuronal connectivity from calcium imaging signals. *PLoS computational biology*,
8(8):e1002653, 2012.

Supervised Neural Network Structure Recovery

Ildefons Magrans de Abril and Ann Nowé

Editors: Demian Battaglia, Isabelle Guyon, Vincent Lemaire, Javier Orlandi, Bisakha Ray and Jordi Soriano

Abstract This paper presents our solution to the European Conference of Machine Learning Neural Connectomics Discovery Challenge. The challenge goal was to improve the performance of existing methods for recovering the neural network structure given the time series of neural activities. We propose to approximate a function able to combine several connectivity indicators between neuron pairs where each indicator is the result of running a feature engineering pipeline optimized for a particular noise level and firing synchronization rate among neurons. We proved the suitability of our solution by improving the state of the art prediction performance more than 6% and by obtaining the third best score on the test dataset out of 144 teams.

Keywords Neural network · Structure recovery · Causality · Time series

1 Introduction

Most advanced neuroimaging techniques, based on calcium sensitive organic dyes (Tsien 1981), are able to capture the in vivo activity of thousands of neurons. This represents a huge improvement with respect to the highly invasive neurophysiol-

The original form of this article appears in JMLR W&CP Volume 46.

I. Magrans de Abril (✉) · A. Nowé
Artificial Intelligence Lab, Vrije Universiteit Brussel, Pleinlaan 2, 1050 Brussels, Belgium
e-mail: Ildefons.Magrans.de.Abril@vub.ac.be

A. Nowé
e-mail: Ann.Nowe@vub.ac.be

ogy multi-electrode recording tools barely capable of recording on the order of 100 neurons. The full potential development of this new instrumentation still requires analysis tools able to infer the underlying topology based on time-series of neuronal activity. The goal of the European Conference of Machine Learning Neural Connectomics Challenge (ChaLearn 2014) was to encourage the application of machine learning techniques to recover the neural network structure using neural activity time-series recordings as input. This paper presents our method[1] to train a regression model that can predict the connectivity between neuron pairs given the time series of neural activities obtained from fluorescence signals. With this solution we obtained the third best score on the test dataset out of 144 teams.

The challenge setup consists of several neural network datasets for both training and testing purposes, an evaluation process, detailed information about the problem and sample code to get started. Neural network datasets consists of one hour time series of neural activities obtained from fluorescence signals sampled at 20 ms intervals with values normalized in the interval [0, 1], information about the position of each neuron in a square area of $1\,mm^2$ and the inter-neuron connectivity labels. The setup evaluation process is built upon the Area Under the ROC Curve (AUC) as evaluation metric and a real-time leaderboard showing the ranking of all teams according to the score obtained on an evaluation dataset. The score on a separated test dataset defined the final ranking of teams. This score was not visible and therefore could not be used to overfit the final model.

There are three major difficulties to detect connectivity among neuron pairs (Stetter et al. 2012): (1) episodes of synchronous bursting conveying low connectivity information, (2) a typical frame video rate is 20 ms which is slower than the neuron's firing dynamic by one order of magnitude and (3) the background has noise.

The challenge sample code has two non-supervised methods: a simple solution based on correlation and a state of the art solution based on the Generalized Transfer Entropy (GTE) indicator (Orlandi et al. 2014; Stetter et al. 2012). The correlation based solution computes the connectivity indicators among 1000 neurons in few minutes without taking into account the causal direction. This naive example was meant uniquely to get as many people as possible started. The C++ implementation of the GTE-based solution is a directional connectivity indicator and it runs in about 12 h on a high-end server. This second solution requires a careful parameter selection and it is a good example of how to score directed connections between neuron pairs taking into account the three major difficulties.

2   Model

The main observation that guided our work was that optimizing a single connectivity indicator, as suggested by the state of the art, may be a limiting strategy because it will tend to work optimally just on a particular regime (i.e. noise level and firing

---

[1]https://github.com/ildefons/connectomics.

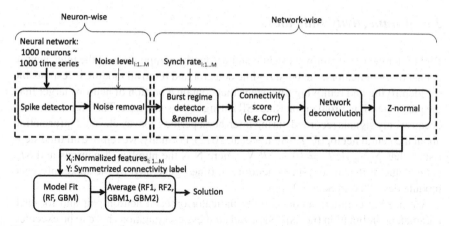

Fig. 1 Solution block diagram. It consists of a feature engineering pipeline to compute several connectivity indicators between each neuron pairs and a model fitting strategy to combine these features

synchronization rate among neurons). Therefore, a function approximation able to optimally combine several indicators, computed using different parameters, should deliver an enhanced performance. This section describes the details of our solution. It consists of a feature engineering pipeline to compute the many connectivity scores according to different parameter values and a suitable model fitting strategy able to combine these features. Figure 1 shows the main components of our solution. The following sub-sections describe in detail each of the building blocks.

2.1 Spike Inference

The first step in our feature engineering pipeline is the spike inference module. It is responsible for inferring spike trains out of time series of neural activities. We have evaluated two approaches: a naive method based on computing the difference between any two consecutive time steps, and a state of the art method (Vogelstein et al. 2009) based on the sequential Monte Carlo framework (a generalization of the Baum–Welch algorithm to fit Hidden Markov Models) that finds the probability of the neuron spiking in each time step.

In both cases, spike trains are post-processed to remove background noise. A parameter named Noise Level (NL) defines the lower limit of a valid spike. Spikes below NL are zeroed. The evaluation of both spike inference methods was performed using the complete solution pipeline outlined in Fig. 1 on a training network (Normal$_1$) constructed similarly to the test network. We analyzed the performance delivered by each method using many different parameters. We finally chose the Monte Carlo framework based method because it delivered a maximum AUC of 0.932 and an average AUC over all parameters of 0.909 while the naive method delivered a maximum AUC of 0.929 and an average AUC over all parameters of 0.902.

2.2 Connectivity Indicators

Right after the noise removal module and before the computation of the inter-neuron connectivity indicators, the burst regime detector and removal module is responsible for identifying and removing time steps that contain a portion of neurons larger than the parameter Synchronization Rate (SR) firing at the same time. This step is required because only signals recorded during inter-burst periods convey elevated information about the neural net topology (Stetter et al. 2012). Formally, we remove all time steps t such that $\sum_{i=1}^{N} \mathbb{1}\{ST_{it} \neq 0\} > SR.N$, where N is the number of neurons and ST_{it} is the value of the spike train of neuron i at time t generated by the spike inference module described in Sect. 2.1.

We need to compute a connectivity indicator on each neuron pair and for each parameter combination (i.e. NL, SR), and all these computations have to be executed for several training networks, the evaluation and the test networks. Therefore, the computation efficiency is a key requirement for this module. Plain correlation was a suitable candidate according to this requirement. Performance-wise, correlation between spike trains delivered a performance equivalent to GTE between pairs of raw time series of neural activity (Orlandi et al. 2014; Stetter et al. 2012).

Correlation is a simple enough connectivity indicator to be able to compute the many indicators using reasonable resources. However, a limitation of using correlation as connectivity indicator is that it is unable to identify directed connections. Therefore, it may not be appropriate when the goal is to identify causal relationships. Fortunately, when the performance evaluation metric is the Area Under the ROC Curve, the added value of distinguishing the connectivity direction is low.

2.3 Network Deconvolution

The final step of the feature engineering pipeline is the network deconvolution module. This module implements a recent network deconvolution algorithm (Feizi et al. 2013) meant to eliminate the combined effect of indirect paths of arbitrary length from an observed correlation matrix containing both direct and indirect effects. This step improves the quality of the connectivity indicators between neuron pairs by taking into account the whole connectivity matrix. This method has been able to improve the performance of state of the art solutions in other network reconstruction application scenarios (Feizi et al. 2013).

This method consists of the following steps: (1) to normalize in the interval [-1, 1] the connectivity indication matrix described in Sect. 2.2, (2) to decompose with SVD the normalized matrix, (3) to compute the eigenvalues of the deconvolved matrix according to $\lambda_i^d = \frac{\lambda_i}{\lambda_i + 1}$ with λ_i being the i_{th} eigenvalue of the normalized matrix, (4) to compose the direct dependency matrix according to $C_{dir} = UDU^{-1}$ where U is a matrix of eigen-vectors and D is a diagonal matrix whose i_{th} diagonal is λ_i^d.

A Z-normalization post-processing delivers a connectivity matrix with a distribution almost identical across different networks using the same parameters (i.e. NL, SR). This additional step is not part of the original deconvolution algorithm. It is motivated by the observation that the deconvolved matrix from any two different neural networks, computed with the same parameter set, had different distributions and therefore they cannot be used directly to train a supervised model.

The evaluation of the network deconvolution step was performed using again the complete solution pipeline outlined in Fig. 1 on a training network (Normal$_1$) constructed similarly to the test network. We analyzed the performance using many different parameters. The deconvolution step improved the maximum performance from 0.911 to 0.932 and the average performance improved from 0.893 to 0.909.

2.4 Modeling Approach

To overcome the limitation of using a single connectivity indicator optimized for a particular noise level and bursting synchronization rate, we propose to approximate a function able to combine several connectivity indicators between neuron pairs. More precisely, given a training network, the set of samples is defined by all possible combinations of different non-directed neuron pairs (e.g. N:Number of network neurons = 1000, number of samples = $\frac{N(N-1)}{2}$ = 499500). Each sample consists of a set of connectivity indicators computed with the feature engineering pipeline described in the previous sections using different parameter values (i.e. NL, SR). Our modeling approach does not try to learn self-loops.

Fitting this function requires a method able to capture complex relationships among several very similar features. Gradient Boosting Machines (GBM) (Ridgeway 2013) and Random Forest (Breiman et al. 2013) have been successfully used in other challenges with similar feature space complexity (Magrans de Abril and Sugiyama 2013). Further concerns were the heterogeneity of the network topologies and the highly imbalanced training network datasets where only approximately 1% of neuron pairs were connected. We minimized the training network topology bias by (1) using a large minimum size for the tree leafs, and (2) averaging four models: two random forest fitted according to two training networks constructed similarly to the test network and two gradient boosting machines models fitted according to the same two networks. We addressed the data imbalance problem by sub-sampling the training samples of non-connected neuron pairs down to 5 times the number of connected neuron pair samples.

3 Evaluation

During the model validation phase, we used three training networks (Normal$_1$, Normal$_2$ and Normal$_3$), the evaluation network and the test network. All networks consists of 1000 neurons and approximately 1% of neuron pairs were connected.

Table 1 Performance results when using the training networks for both model fitting and testing purposes. The row labels define the network under test and column labels define the predictive model (e.g. GTE $\sim$ Generalized Transfer Entropy, $R_1 + G_1 \sim$ average of RF and GBM both fitted with network$_1$, ALL $\sim$ average of RF and GBM both fitted with the two other networks not being tested as proposed in Sect. 2.4)

T	GTE	R_1	G_1	R_2	G_2	R_3	G_3	$R_1 + G_1$	$R_2 + G_2$	$R_3 + G_3$	ALL
N_1	0.885	NA	NA	0.9392	0.9388	0.9394	0.9386	NA	0.9398	0.9398	0.9401
N_2	0.889	0.9399	0.9401	NA	NA	0.9403	0.9399	0.9409	NA	0.9409	0.9413
N_3	0.884	0.9393	0.9396	0.9392	0.9396	NA	NA	0.9402	0.9402	NA	0.9405

According to the challenge data description, all these networks were constructed similarly. For each network we extracted a number of connectivity indicator matrices. Each connectivity matrix was computed running the feature engineering pipeline described in Sect. 2 with a given parameter set (i.e. NL, SR). More precisely, for each network we computed 252 matrices according to all possible parameters set combinations where:

$NL \in \{0.07, 0.075, 0.08, 0.085, 0.09, 0.1, 0.11, 0.12, 0.13, 0.14, 0.15, 0.16, 0.17, 0.18\}$

$SR \in \{25, 50, 75, 100, 150, 200, 250, 300, 350, 400, 450, 500, 550, 600, 650, 700, 750, 800\}$

For each training network (e.g. Normal$_1$), we trained a RF and a GBM. To cope with inconsistencies among networks, we used a large minimum size for the tree leafs (450 for RF, 400 for GBM).

Table 1 shows the performance results when using the training networks for both model fitting and testing purposes. Column 1 shows the performance obtained with the state of the art solution (i.e. Generalized Transfer Entropy indicator Orlandi et al. 2014; Stetter et al. 2012). Column 2 to 7 show the prediction performance when we use a single RF or GBM trained with one training network. It shows that our supervised modeling approach is able to reliably deliver a superior performance compared to the best individual connectivity indicator. For instance, RF$_2$ to predict the connectivity of Normal$_1$ network delivers a prediction performance of 0.9392 while the best individual connectivity indicator computed with our feature engineering pipeline delivers a performance of 0.932 and an optimized connectivity indicator computed with GTE delivers a performance of 0.889.

Column 8 to 10 show the prediction performance when we average the predictions delivered by RF and GBM trained with one training network. They show experimental evidence that by averaging the predictions of several models we were able to further improve the prediction performance. From these 3 columns we can also conclude that there is not a training network that provides a superior performance (e.g. training on Normal$_1$ and testing on Normal$_2$ delivers a performance of 0.9409 and training on Normal$_3$ and testing on Normal$_2$ delivers the same performance of 0.9409). Finally, column 11 shows the prediction performance when we average the

Table 2 Performance results when using the training networks for both model fitting and testing purposes. The row labels define the network under test and column labels define the the the random seed used to sub-sample training samples of non-connected neuron pairs. All prediction models are computed according to Sect. 2.4

Test	$Seed_1$	$Seed_2$	$Seed_3$
$Normal_1$	0.94007	0.94009	0.94009
$Normal_2$	0.94134	0.94129	0.94121
$Normal_3$	0.94051	0.94053	0.94048

predictions delivered by RF and GBM trained with the two other training networks as proposed in Sect. 2.4.

Table 2 presents the performance results when using the training networks to fit a complete model according to the description of Sect. 2.4 (i.e. last column of Table 1) and using different random seeds before the sub-sampling of non-connected neuron pair samples. The row labels define the network under test and the column labels define the random seed applied before sub-sampling. It shows that sub-sampling has a very small effect on the model performance. Therefore, we are unlikely losing much information.

Finally, a model trained with $Normal_1$ and $Normal_2$ delivered a performance on the test network of 0.9406 which is 0.06 higher than the performance obtained with the best known solution before the challenge started (i.e. Generalized Transfer Entropy (GTE) indicator Orlandi et al. 2014; Stetter et al. 2012).

4 Conclusions and Future Work

Our modeling hypothesis is that by approximating a function able to optimally combine several indicators, computed using different parameters (i.e. noise level and firing synchronization rate among neurons), we could deliver an enhanced performance. The feature engineering pipeline is responsible for the computation of the connectivity indicators. It is based on a modular design able to separately address the different difficulties to detect connectivity among neuron pairs: (1) episodes of synchronous bursting conveying low connectivity information, (2) a typical frame video rate is 20 ms which is slower than the neuron's firing dynamic by one order of magnitude and (3) the background has noise. We have proven the suitability of our solution by improving the state of the art prediction performance (AUC) in more than 6% and by obtaining the third best score on the test dataset out of 144 teams.

However, we believe that there is still room for improvement. For instance, important functional limitations of our model are that it is unable to identify the connectivity directions and self-loops. We also believe that there exist possibilities to improve our model such as using a finer grained grid of parameters or by using semi-supervised variants of RF (Leistner et al. 2009) and GBM (Dai et al. 2007).

Table 3 Summary table with team name, final private leaderboard performance and performance of the winner

Team name	Ildefons Magrans
Private leaderboard performance	0.94063
Performance of the winner	0.94161

Another limitation of our method is a high computational cost mainly due to the large number of connectivity indicators on several training networks and the test network. More precisely, the many correlation matrix and the SVD step during the network deconvolution have a computational complexity on the order of $O(MKNn^2)$ and $O(MKn^3)$ respectively, where n is the number of neurons (1000), N is the number of time steps (180000), K is the number of connectivity indicators (252) and M is the number of networks (3). Running on an i7 quad core laptop with 32 Gbytes of RAM, it takes 48 h to compute the connectivity indicators for all networks, just below 5 h to compute the spike trains and just above 2 h to fit the random forest and the GBM models.

Acknowledgements Ildefons Magrans de Abril and Ann Nowé were supported by EU FP7 framework's Marie Curie Industry-Academia Partnerships and Pathways (IAPP) project SCANERGY, under grant agreement number 324321.

Appendix A. Result Table

See Table 3.

References

Leo Breiman, Adele Cutler, Andy Liaw, and Matthew Wiener. R package randomforest: Breiman and cutler's random forests for classification and regression. Version 4.6–7, 2013.

ChaLearn. Connectomics challenge. http://connectomics.chalearn.org/, 2014.

Wenyuan Dai, Qiang Yang, Gui-Rong Xue, and Yong Yu. Boosting for transfer learning. In *Proceedings of the 24th international conference on Machine learning*, pages 193–200. ACM, 2007.

Soheil Feizi, Daniel Marbach, Muriel Médard, and Manolis Kellis. Network deconvolution as a general method to distinguish direct dependencies in networks. *Nature biotechnology*, 31(8): 726–733, 2013.

Christian Leistner, Amir Saffari, Jakob Santner, and Horst Bischof. Semi-supervised random forests. In *Computer Vision, 2009 IEEE 12th International Conference on*, pages 506–513. IEEE, 2009.

Ildefons Magrans de Abril and Masashi Sugiyama. Winning the kaggle algorithmic trading challenge with the composition of many models and feature engineering. *IEICE Transactions on Information and Systems*, 96(3):742–745, 2013.

Javier G. Orlandi, Olav Stetter, Jordi Soriano, Theo Geisel, and Demian Battaglia. Transfer entropy reconstruction and labeling of neuronal connections from simulated calcium imaging. arXiv:1309.4287v2, May 2014.

Greg Ridgeway. R package gbm: Generalized boosted regression models. Version 2.1, 2013.

Olav Stetter, Demian Battaglia, Jordi Soriano, and Theo Geisel. Model-free reconstruction of excitatory neuronal connectivity from calcium imaging signals. *PLOS Computational Biology*, 8(8), August 2012.

R.Y. Tsien. A non-disruptive technique for loading calcium buffers and indicators into cells. *Nature*, 290: 527–528, April 1981.

Joshua T. Vogelstein, Brendon O. Watson, Adam M. Packer, Rafael Yuste, Bruno Jedynako, and Liam Paninski. Spike inference from calcium imaging using sequential monte carlo methods. *Biophysical journal*, 97(2):636–655, 2009.

Signal Correlation Prediction Using Convolutional Neural Networks

Lukasz Romaszko

Editors: Demian Battaglia, Isabelle Guyon, Vincent Lemaire,
Javier Orlandi, Bisakha Ray, Jordi Soriano

Abstract This paper focuses on analysing multiple time series relationships such as correlations between them. We develop a deep learning solution for the Connectiomics contest dataset of fluorescence imaging of neural activity recordings – the aim is reconstruction of the wiring between brain neurons. The model makes accurate predictions and took the fourth place in this contest. The performance is similar to the other leading solutions, thus we showed that deep learning methods for time series processing are comparable to the other approaches and have wide opportunities for further improvement. We discuss a range of methods and technical details relevant to our convolutional neural network for the time series domain.

Keywords Deep learning · Convolutional neural network · Multiple time series · Classification · Correlation · Connectome

1 Introduction

We implement a model involving a deep learning approach suitable for multiple time series processing (Bengio 2009). The developed model is evaluated on the dataset of fluorescence imaging of neural activity recordings for connection prediction, prepared for the machine learning contest hosted on the kaggle.com platform. The

---

The original form of this article appears in JMLR W&CP Volume 46.

L. Romaszko (✉)
University of Edinburgh, Edinburgh, UK
e-mail: lukasz.romaszko@gmail.com

© Springer International Publishing AG 2017
D. Battaglia et al. (eds.), *Neural Connectomics Challenge*, The Springer Series
on Challenges in Machine Learning, DOI 10.1007/978-3-319-53070-3_4

contest, entitled *Connectomics*, was organized by ChaLearn[1] in spring 2014. Understanding the exact brain structure is crucial for research on brain functioning and its learning capabilities. Therefore the aim of the Connectomics is reconstruction of the wiring between brain neurons, which is achieved by estimating the correlations of all pairs of cells (i.e. neurons in a real brain) in the provided network.

2　Dataset and Evaluation

The Brain dataset of neural network recordings comes from a simulator (Stetter et al. 2012). The organisers provided several networks, the most important are: four Normal networks for training, Validation and Test for prediction, each composed of $N = 1000$ cells. Another type of networks were 6 Small networks, composed of 100 cells. They required 100 times lower number of predictions, therefore they were good for fast verification purposes. The length of the activity recordings in all the networks is 180, 000 frames, which represent one hour simulation with a 20 ms frame rate. This frame rate is very low, which makes this task a real challenge. The ground-truth answer is a binary matrix of ones and zeros. The graph is sparse – the edges constitute 1% of all possible connections. The prediction is a matrix of N^2 values between 0 and 1, indicating a confidence that there is a connection between given cells. For this binary classification task the standard Area Under the Receiver Operating Characteristic (ROC) curve scoring measure was used (denoted by AUC). ROC is a graphical plot that illustrates the performance of a binary classifier, when applying all possible thresholds. It compares the order of the predicted confidence with the expected one. It is worth emphasising that the AUC score ranges from 0.5 (random prediction) to 1.0 (ideal prediction). In this contest, for the specifics of the Normal networks structure, which is sparse (connections are 1% of all possible edges), the score of 0.8, is not satisfactory. The score of 0.9, even though close to 1.0, would still mean that after applying an optimal threshold there would be more false positive than true positive connections.

The most important for connection detection is communication, which means that the recorded signals have spikes at similar time. It is worth emphasising that the baseline Cross-correlation solution is using only this observation. In all of the described approaches we assume that an activity recording is a discrete derivative of the original values of the fluorescence signal of a recorded cell. Therefore, a single cell's activity value at the time frame i is: $recording_i = FluorescenceRecording_{i+1} - FluorescenceRecording_i$. Thus, the value of recording (discrete derivative) equal to 0 means no change in the activity level of the given cell. In the provided dataset the activity recording values range from around -0.2 (a drop) to 1.0 (a spike). The absolute value of a drop is much lower than the one of a spike, since the substance can quickly increase its brightness when provided an input, but then substance brightness decays slowly.

[1]http://www.chalearn.org/.

3   CNN Model

Before proceeding to developing a complex CNN model, we tested a simpler, but a very promising solution. The learning method used in the solution is straightforward: each input is encoded into a finite space, with very similar inputs encoded to the same value. The method remembers the number of positive and negative examples of that particular encoded value. Therefore it is a simple pattern recogniser, a mock of a CNN.

3.1   The First Solution: Basic Approach

The idea behind the method of connection prediction within a pair is to take fragments of activity recordings (two fragments of recording covering the same period of time, each from one cell) in order to compute the probability that cells with these exact fragments are connected. To have a limited number of possible inputs, values of the recordings were discretised into 4 integer values, representing a drop, no change, a small increase and a spike. The threshold of a spike and increase (0.3, 0.1) was close to the Cross-correlation baseline threshold of a spike (0.2), the three thresholds splitting the values into 4 intervals for discretisation were as follows: -0.05, 0.1, 0.3. The length of one fragment was set to 6, to not exceed the memory allocation limits. Thus the recordings were represented by 4 different possible values, in total 2 fragments, each fragment of length 6 (total input length equals $2 \cdot 6 = 12$). This led to 4^{12} combinations, which is around 17 million different possible inputs. The input values were encoded into 64-bit integer, stored in two 17-million elements arrays, representing their #pos and #neg counts. The code was converted to C using Cython library,[2] a Python framework for direct translation of a Python code (with previously assigned types to variables) to C. This decreased execution time by more than one order of magnitude.

A probability of a pair being connected, based only by its two 6-length signal values, was defined by the number of positive occurrences in the training dataset (number of cases that such a pair was connected), #pos, and the negative number of this particular case, #neg. The confidence was then straightforwardly $\frac{\#pos}{\#pos+\#neg}$ for the given case of activity recording. The final confidence for a given directed connection was calculated as an average of the above confidences through all possible time shifts. We tested the performance of the Basic Approach on 6 Small networks of 100 cells by comparing the result to the accuracy of cross-correlation. In Fig. 1 we present a comparison of both methods, showing that the Basic Approach outperforms Cross-correlation baseline provided by the organisers. Our Basic Approach is better, since it takes into account longer patterns, instead of basing the prediction on pairs of single values. The Basic Approach is better on average by 3.25 percentage point.

---

[2]http://www.cython.org/.

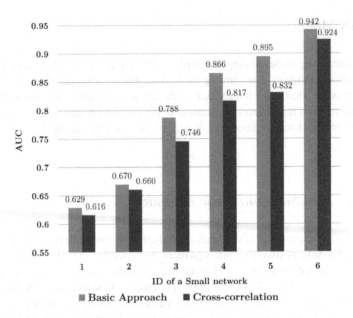

Fig. 1 Basic approach compared to cross-correlation

The method is simple, however the implementation of optimisations for Cython took significant amount of time. Despite its simplicity, on the Normal networks the presented Basic Approach received 90.0% AUC score. It outperforms the baselines (88.3 and 89.3%). Eventually, together with frame filtering keeping periods of a high activity of the whole network, which we describe later, the Basic Approach obtained a score of 90.6%, and would be classified in top 20% of all the submitted solutions.

3.2 Background on Convolutional Neural Networks

In this section we will present a brief discussion of basics of convolutional neural networks. They constitute the core of our solution, so we describe their structure properties in detail. Finally, we present Max-pooling, which is a technique that helps to improve learning.

3.2.1 Convolutional Neural Networks

A commonly known, standard feed-forward fully connected Neural Network (NN) is a computational model composed of several layers, where each layer has several neurons (units). An input to a particular unit are outputs of all the units in the previous layer (or input data for the first layer). The unit output is a single linear regression, to which output value a specific activation function is applied. Convolutional neural network (CNN) is a type of NN where the input variables are related spatially to each other. In a standard NN, a permutation (constant for the whole computation) of input variables does not change the final accuracy of the NN, since the model treats them equivalently. However, to detect for example patterns or objects in images, the input (e.g. pixels order in an image) cannot be permuted, since that will lose spatial dependencies. To take into account very important spatial positions, CNNs were developed. Not only they are able to detect general spatial dependencies, but also are capable of specific patterns recognition. Shared weights, representing different patterns, improve the convergence by reducing significantly the number of parameters. CNN recognise small patterns at each layer, generalising them (detecting higher order, more complex patterns) in subsequent layers. Usually a small filter of a particular pattern is applied with all possible shifts to an image. This means that to compute an output (called a feature map) a layer uses the same filter, defined by its weights. This allows detection of various patterns and keeps the number of weights to be learned very low.

3.2.2 Convolutional Layer Details

A convolutional layer belongs to a CNN and is determined in particular by the number of filters and their shapes it can learn to recognise patterns. It takes as input fragments of feature maps produced in the previous layer. Usually, layers are fully-connected, which means that next layer filters over all the maps from the previous layer. The feature map dimension depends on the input dimension as well as on the filter shape. The filter is applied to all the possible shifts in the previous map, thus the new dimension is the input dimension decreased by the filter dimension. For instance, for an input [50 × 50] and filter shape [2 × 10], the new feature map is [49 × 41]. When we say that convolutional layers has N units, it means that each of these N units is generating a 2-dimensional feature map, resulting in N 2-dimensional feature maps passed as the output.

3.2.3 Max-Pooling

To improve learning, the concept of max-pooling (Boureau et al. 2010) has been developed. To decrease the size of an obtained feature map, it is divided into rectangles (pools), in image recognition usually into squares [$k \times k$] where $k \in \{2, 3, 4, 5\}$. Only the highest activation value of a unit, i.e. a maximal value within the respective rectangle is preserved. It allows to reduce the size of intermediate representation by k^2 in a single layer. Max-pooling keeps information about the highest matching to the given pattern among the units within a respective pool, so the information whether a certain pattern was detected in a given small region is persisted, which is the most

important in pattern recognition. While learning, the errors are only propagated to
the position of the maximally activated unit.

3.3 Introduction to CNN Filter and CNN Model

The Basic Approach method had disadvantages due to a significant information loss,
therefore we decided to use CNN which are often the best state-of-the-art models
for pattern recognition (Ciresan et al. 2012). We based our initial CNN structure
on the network called Lenet5, which is a CNN designed for digit recognition by
LeCun (LeCun et al. 1998). That network achieves an error rate below 0.9% in the
MNIST dataset. We adapted an implementation of Lenet5 for our task of time series
processing. Our CNN is composed of five layers: three convolutional layers, then one
fully connected standard layer and Softmax. The Softmax function is commonly used
for the classification. It maps n-length input into c classes, the output are probabilities
of each class. In our case the Softmax layer has two outputs, one for negative and
one for positive class. In this paper by $[N \times M]$ we denote a 2-dimensional matrix.
It has N rows, each of a length M. $[K \times N \times M]$ denotes K 2-dimensional matrices.
A *Unit* is the another name for a neuron in a CNN.

The learning was performed using 1.2 million of examples, 96% of which were
used to learn and 4% to evaluate accuracy of the network during learning. From
now on we assume that training is performed using one of the Normal brain network
recordings (network: *Normal1*). The number of positive and negative examples is
equal, even in the network they are in the ratio 1 to 100. Moreover, all pairs were
included the same number of times in their class – for example, if there are 10, 000
connected pairs, and we want 30, 000 examples in the training dataset, we create 3
examples composed of signals of each pair, starting at different time. The time-shift,
i.e. a frame which fragment starts at, for each example was chosen uniformly at
random. This condition is important since if all pairs started in some selected frame,
e.g. in the first, the network would overfit to match positions of spikes. Learning
was performed by optimisation of all CNN weights by Gradient Descent algorithm
(LeCun et al. 1998). Below, we refer to a trained CNN as to the *CNN Filter*, since it
predicts a probability based on a partial input. The CNN Model is a whole solution of
data pre-processing, training and prediction. Within it, the CNN Filter is applied to
a pair of fragments of recordings, alike in the Basic Approach. Figure 2 presents the
simplified workflow of our solution. In the CNN Model, a final confidence prediction
for a particular pair is an average probability, assessed by applying the CNN Filter
to different periods of recordings, shifted each time by a constant number of frames,
covering the whole input. A single *pass* is an evaluation of all the pairs starting in a
given time frame. We perform a few passes for each pair. The number of passes could
by arbitrary, but at least should cover the whole input. For the provided networks the
minimal number was 5 (the length of input after the filtering was 1500, while CNN
Filter length was 330). However, assessing the input in equal shifts would cause that

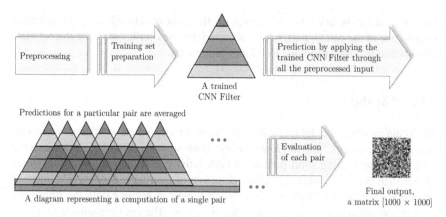

Fig. 2 CNN Model - simplified workflow

some parts of the input would be assessed twice, and other parts only once. Increasing the number of passes improves the accuracy and makes the number of assessments more uniform, finally we perform 14 passes, since we tested that was comparable with the higher number of passes.

3.4   CNN Filter Key Time Series Processing Methods

3.4.1   Spatial Representation

The initial idea was to incorporate time information by providing fragments in a two-dimensional matrix ($[2 \times length]$). To take into consideration these time dependencies while learning, filters in the first layer cover both recordings simultaneously. The detected patterns are then combined in the next, higher level layers. In addition to the two rows representing a pair of signals, a third row was computed. It was computed during the pre-processing, based on the whole network data and each time added to the two rows as an additional feature. This row includes overall (the whole) network activity increase in a respective frame. The overall activity is defined as: the total change in the network activity, which equals to the sum of activity recordings of all cells in a respective frame. This allows the CNN filter to learn the network different behaviour depending on its activity level. This led to a major improvement in accuracy, since it significantly enhances distinguishing different states of a network. We tested that applying two filters of height 2, and subsequently again a filter of height 2 in the next layer gave much better result, than just a filter of height 3 in the first layer. CNN was able to learn simple patterns and then predict more accurately by learning their combinations in the second layer. Also, better results were achieved when the second layer had more units (number of combinations) than when more

units were set in the first layer. Moreover, the third row of network activity is adjacent
only to one of the cell signals, which occurred that was sufficient, since the network
already had that data provided to infer dependencies.

3.4.2 Filtering

The brain time series exhibit two regimes: high activity, when an external input was
given to the network, and the low activity, when signal amplitudes are low, mixed
with the noise. During short periods of high activity, cells activity is several times
higher than normally, which enhances detection of interdependencies. The method
of filtering performed during pre-processing consist in keeping only the fragments
of high overall activity, above a particular threshold. The cut fragments were glued
together in their appearing order. This method reduces the frames number, in our
case, to only around 1% of the initial number of frames in the provided dataset.
The threshold value of 20 (which means that the average of activity recordings in
that frame is higher than 0.02) was selected based on local validation. This parameter had to be chosen purely by local validation, moreover, increasing the threshold
value preserves even more active time frames (increases accuracy) but the input data
amount is smaller (decreases accuracy). Lowering this parameters changes the above
properties in the opposite way, which to a certain extent reduce themselves and the
accuracy is similar. Therefore the exact value was not that important, the most important was preserving only the most active fragments, i.e. around 1% of the total input.
Without filtering, the communication is very rare, and CNN would not be able to
learn properly (since in many positive examples there would be no communication
in the non-filtered recordings).

3.4.3 Proper Activation Functions

One of the important decisions related to CNN was setting proper activation functions
in the units. We started with the default hyperbolic tangent (tanh, $\lambda x. \frac{e^{2x}-1}{e^{2x}+1}$) activation
function, afterwards tested other ones. Finally, the most common one, tanh activation
function is used in first convolutional layer, while Rectified Linear Unit (ReLU,
$\lambda x. \max(0, x)$) in the next two convolutional layers. The latter activation function
is often suggested as closer to biological behaviour (Nair and Hinton 2010). Since
positive indications of correlation should be additive it occurred that using ReLU
improved the result. Indeed, ReLU's additive behaviour can improve the positive
patterns detection. The stronger the matching of a filter pattern, the linearly higher
the output (contrary to a tanh activation), while in an accidental case when an input
is a negative of the filter pattern, the output is 0, hence disregarded (contrary to a
linear activation).

3.4.4 Improvement of the CNN Filter

The data was normalised (mean 0, standard deviation 1), what increased learning speed. The same normalisation factors, saved during pre-processing training dataset, were used when normalising test networks.

Afterwards, we substantially improved the network structure. Firstly, we did not apply max-pooling in the first two layers, since the frequency was low compared to cells communication speed. We wanted to keep all the available information, which was already in very low resolution. However, we used max pooling in the last convolutional layer, with a rather high information loss, of length 10 ([1 × 10]). It allowed to select most interesting cases, i.e. to update the weights based on the correlations indication, which had a much higher probability of occurring in the 10-length span. Max-pooling should allow to update the network parameters according to those true correlation indicators. Since the errors are only propagated to the position of the maximally activated unit, it is highly probable that in a wider span there will exist a strong indication of a communication between cells, especially since the data is composed of a high activity periods. Gradient Descent (hereafter GD) will calculate the derivative only based on the maximal ones, thus a possible correlation indicators, on the contrary of performing it based on each input value and regardless its relevance.

Another method applied to improve learning, was momentum (Polyak 1964). GD performs steps based on the derivative which has a dimension of a number of parameters and updates each respective parameter independently. With the momentum, GD algorithm updates are based mainly on the previous one, refreshed according to the current gradient. This method allows avoiding local extrema, since a few wrong gradients will not affect the final step direction. We could explain the momentum by a physical movement: when using the momentum, GD steps over time act like a velocity, whilst gradient updates like an acceleration.

3.5 CNN Filter Structure

After presenting all the aforementioned crucial CNN features, we can describe the exact setup of the CNN structure. The number of frames passed to the input is 330. This number was selected based on local validation and the available memory limit, to keep the input length and dataset size high but balanced. The input length, changed within a range of 200 to 400 is almost not influencing the final result, since decreasing (slightly) the length by a factor p (decreases accuracy) would allow a p times larger dataset size for training (increases accuracy). This length of 330 covers around 20% of total simulation time after frame-filtering. The first two rows are cell signals, the third row is overall network activity, which results in an input of 3 by 330 dimension. The network parameters were chosen to get the highest score when tested on Normal

Table 1 CNN Filter details. A.F. denotes activation function. Outgoing dimensions is passed to the next layer. Layer 3 has last outgoing dimension equal to 32 due to max pooling, i.e. 322 div 10 = 32

#	Layer type	Units	A.F.	Max-pool.	Filter shape	Outgoing dimensions
0	Input	–	–	–	–	(input) [3 × 330]
1	Convolutional	18	tanh	None	[1 × 2 × 5]	[18 × 2 × 326]
2	Convolutional	40	ReLU	None	[18 × 2 × 5]	[40 × 1 × 322]
3	Convolutional	15	ReLU	[1 × 10]	[40 × 1 × 1]	[15 × 1 × 32]
4	Standard	100	tanh	–	–	[100]
5	Softmax	–	–	–	–	(output, 2 classes) [2]

networks. Finally, the subsequent network layers are presented in Table 1. Please note that number of units in convolutional layers equals their feature maps number.

The final structure can be inferred from Fig. 3, which also presents some extra visualisations, e.g. the small green square represents a single value in a single feature map, calculated by applying a filter of [18 × 2 × 5] weights (which are this feature map's parameters to be learned during training) to all of the feature maps in the previous layer. Regarding learning settings, the learning rate was set to 0.05, linearly decreasing to 0.01; momentum to 0.5, increasing to almost 1.0 in the last epoch.

To improve the final result we computed 8 separate outputs (Krogh and Vedelsby 1995) using different seeds for the random number generator. These outputs where aggregated by averaging predicted values of each pair. It occurred that using two times more outputs for averaging increases the final score by a slightly more than 0.1 percentage point. Since one output was around 93.6%, two outputs gave around 93.7%, four 93.85% and finally eight the result close to 94.0%, which increased the initial score by almost 0.4 percentage point.

3.6 On the CNN Model Implementation and Development

Architecture and performance The code is written in Python, using the Numerical Python (NumPy) library for numerical operations. To allow parallel execution of the code on a graphic card's GPU (Graphics Processing Unit), we use Python library, Theano. Execution was performed on a fast graphic card nVidia K20 with 5 GB memory on board. A computation of one epoch, which processes over one million examples, lasts about 30 min. Number of epochs was set to 20, so it took around 10 h for the training process. Total execution time for the whole workflow was 15 h. Please note that in one CNN Model run, we evaluate four networks, each by performing 14 passes. This leads to a huge number of 56 million CNN Filter applications, each composed of thousands of computations.

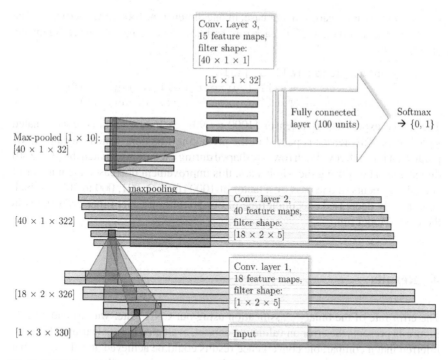

Fig. 3 CNN structure

Spatial representation optimisation An important major improvement regarding implementation is how to perform fast creation of pairs in Theano, without copying the values. The input dimension is [3 × 330], two signals and activity level row. One pass is composed of 1000 iterations (batches), where each batch is assessing 1000 pairs (input examples). Even if the model computation for a given pair is optimised, the significant time is wasted for preparing the input for CNN Filter by storing the input values directly. We solved this problem in the following way: instead of copying all triples of fragments, we stored the data in a form of three columns (tensors), each column with 1000 rows, each row of length 330. All cells signal values for that particular pass is denoted by `all_signals`. The second column is a tile of a cell's signal fragment, `current_cell_signal`. In one iteration we assess all connections incoming to that cell. The value of `current_cell_signal` is updated in each iteration. The third column is composed of `network_act`, network overall activity row, also tiled. T denotes `Theano.Tensor` module, `T.horizontal_stack()` concatenates given rows and `T.tile()` virtually copies (tiles) a row given number of times in two dimensions, in our case, in one dimension, 1000 times vertically. The result is an array [1000 × 330], each row with the same values. All three fragments are joined by:

```
T.horizontal_stack (all_signals,
                    T.tile(current_cell_signal, (1000, 1)),
                    T.tile(network_act, (1000, 1))).
```

The above expression is a tensor [1000 × 990], each row of three concatenated signal rows. This tensor is passed to the predicting function, which executes CNN prediction for each row. Each row is reshaped during execution to match the [3 × 330] dimension. Thus during the whole pass, this improvement decreased the number of copied fragments in one pass by a factor of 1000 (from 2, 001, 000 to 2001), which significantly decreased execution time of our 56 million CNN Filter evaluations in the CNN Model run.

4 Results

The error rate of the binary classification using our CNN Filter was around 12.5%. Figure 4a presents the error on validation dataset, evaluated during learning. It can be inferred that a comparable convergence results could be achieved at 7-th epoch, but we aimed to increase the accuracy as much as possible. Figure 4b presents the score obtained by the CNN Model trained through a particular number of epochs. After 10-th epoch the accuracy increases very slowly, therefore we stop training after 20 epochs. There is no overfitting since the number of parameters is moderate compared to the 1.2 million examples in the training dataset due to shared weights. It would be

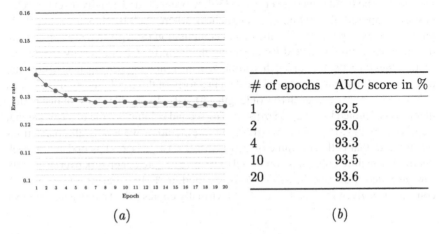

# of epochs	AUC score in %
1	92.5
2	93.0
4	93.3
10	93.5
20	93.6

(a)   (b)

Fig. 4 a Error rate on a validation set through 20 epochs of learning. **b** The AUC score obtained after training the model through a particular number of epochs

Table 2 Results – comparison of our solutions and top Contest solutions

Solution	AUC score in %
1st place (Team: AAAGV)	94.2
Our CNN Model (4th place, team: Lukasz 8000)	94.0
10th place	92.8
Our Basic Approach (with the filtering)	90.6
30th place	90.4
Baseline: GTE	89.3
Baseline: Cross-correlation	88.3

not reasonable to run the training much longer, since better results could be achieved by an average of two predictions instead of an output generated by one model trained two times longer.

The result of a single run of our CNN Model was 93.6%, and averaging the 8 outputs increased the accuracy from 93.6 to 94.0%. The score of 94.0% is therefore the final Contest result. The final results of the contest are presented in Table 2. The CNN Model significantly outperforms the baselines: Cross-correlation (AUC score 88.3%) and Generalised Transfer Entropy (score 89.3%), as well as our Basic Approach (90.6%). Our Model took the fourth place in the Contest out of 144 teams, achieving accuracy comparable to the other top solutions, where the best solution achieved 94.2% AUC score. On the Validation network the solution took the third place. Since the differences between the results of the top solutions were marginal, we can expect that further exploration of deep learning methods can outperform signal processing techniques.

5   Conclusions

It is worth emphasising that we developed a pure deep learning solution. Incorporation of signal pre-processing methods into our approach might significantly improve its performance. We would get also a higher score, when more outputs were used for averaging. To conclude, the results are promising, especially because deep learning methods are often the best current state-of-the-art approaches in pattern recognition. Due to CNNs complexity, these models provide a wide range of possibilities of further enhancement and additional experiments. Since such models could outperform current methods in various domains of time series analysis, their more in-depth inspection is left for prospective research.

References

Y. Bengio. Learning deep architectures for ai. *Foundations and Trends in Machine Learning, volume 2, iss. 1, pages 1–127,* 2009.

Y. Boureau, J. Ponce, and Y. Lecun. A theoretical analysis of feature pooling in visual recognition. *ICML 2010, page 111–118, Omnipress,* 2010.

D.C. Ciresan, U. Meier, and J. Schmidhuber. Multi-column deep neural networks for image classification. *CoRR, Volume abs/1202.2745,* 2012.

A. Krogh and J. Vedelsby. Neural network ensembles, cross validation, and active learning,. *Advances in Neural Information Processing Systems, volume 7, pages 231–238. MIT Press, 1995,* 1995.

Y. LeCun, L. Bottou, Y. Bengio, and P. Haffner. Gradient-based learning applied to document recognition. *Proceedings of the IEEE, 86, pages 2278–2324,* 1998.

V. Nair and G.E. Hinton. Rectified linear units improve restricted boltzmann machines. *In Proceedings of ICML. 2010, pages 807–814,* 2010.

B. T. Polyak. Some methods of speeding up the convergence of iteration methods. *USSR Computational Mathematics and Mathematical Physics, 4(5):1–17,* 1964.

O. Stetter, D. Battaglia, J. Soriano, and T. Geisel. Model-free reconstruction of excitatory neuronal connectivity from calcium imaging signals. *PLOS Computational Biology, August 2012, Volume 8, Issue 8,* 2012.

Reconstruction of Excitatory Neuronal Connectivity via Metric Score Pooling and Regularization

Chenyang Tao, Wei Lin and Jianfeng Feng

Editors: Demian Battaglia, Isabelle Guyon, Vincent Lemaire,
Javier Orlandi, Bisakha Ray, Jordi Soriano

Abstract Unravelling the causal link of neuronal pairs has considerable impacts in neuroscience, yet it still remains a major challenge. Recent investigations in the literature show that the Generalized Transfer Entropy (GTE), derived from information theory, has a great capability of reconstructing the underlying connectomics. In this work, we first generalize the GTE to a measure called Csiszár's Transfer Entropy (CTE). With a proper choice of the convex function, the CTE outperforms the GTE in connectomic reconstruction, especially in the synchronized bursting regime where the GTE was reported to have poor sensitivity. Akin to the ensemble learning approach, we then pool various measures to achieve cutting edge neuronal network connectomic reconstruction performance. As a final step emphasize the importance of introducing regularization schemes in the network reconstruction.

Keywords Csiszár's transfer entropy · Metric score pooling · Network regularization · Inverse correlation

The original form of this article appears in JMLR W&CP Volume 46.

C. Tao · W. Lin
Centre for Computational Systems Biology and School of Mathematical Sciences,
Fudan University, Shanghai, China
e-mail: cytao@fudan.edu.cn

W. Lin
e-mail: wlin@fudan.edu.cn

J. Feng (✉)
Department of Computer Science, The University of Warwick, Coventry, UK
e-mail: jianfeng64@gmail.com

1 Introduction

Understanding the structure and mechanism of the human brain at the cellular and subcellular levels has long been the most challenging issue of science, as echoed in both the recent USA BRAIN project and the EU HBP project. Such a deep understanding will reveal the functions of brain and further inspire the development of the diagnosis, treatment and prognoses of major neurological disorders, such as Alzheimer's disease. We note that recent investigations usually start from understanding learning capability - one of the prominent features of the brain. It is therefore a key issue to reliably recover both the exact wiring patten and the wiring strength of the network at the neuronal level; these are tightly associated with the learning capability of the brain, as the result of the Hebbian learning rule and spike time-dependent plasticities.

Although the traditional neuroanatomic method of axonal tracing can characterize the connectivity for some very small networks, it cannot be applied directly to networks with large scales. Recent advances in calcium imaging has provided an alternative for unveiling the complex neuronal circuitry (Grienberger and Konnerth 2012). Optical imaging of neuronal activity makes it possible to monitor the simultaneous activity of tens of thousands of neurons, with a time resolution of 20 ms. With the help of computational algorithms, the causal relationship between neuronal pairs can be determined and the corresponding large scale of the neuronal network reconstructed (Stetter et al. 2012).

To advance research on neuron network reconstruction from Calcium fluorescence imaging data, a platform calling participants to compare and improve their network reconstruction algorithms was established by the committee of 2014 Connectomics Challenge. Synthetic calcium fluorescence recordings generated from realistically simulated neuronal network were presented to the participants to reconstruct synaptic wiring. A few samples, with ground truth topology, were provided to train participants' models, one validation set without ground truth topology was provided to validate their solutions, and the performances of the solutions were benchmarked on a test sample using the so-called Area Under ROC Curve (AUC) score. In this short paper, we introduce our approach for solving the challenge, which finally ranks 9th on the platform.

The remainder of this paper is organized as follows. In Sect. 2, we first describe the preprocessing steps adopted, then we detail the CTE measure, score pooling and regularization procedure. The results are presented in Sect. 3. Finally in Sect. 4, we discuss the limitations of our approach and point out a few potential future directions.

2 Methods

2.1 Preprocessing of Calcium Imaging

The following preprocessing steps have been adopted to generate input data for computing the metric scores used in the reconstruction of neuronal wiring.

Two schemes have been used to separate the synchronized and unsynchronized dynamical regimes. First one is simple thresholding, the period during which mean Calcium imaging intensity exceeding certain threshold is identified as synchronized bursting regime. Multiple thresholding parameters are used (from 0.12 to 0.25). The second approach explicitly extracts the synchronized dynamics and deflates it from the individual recordings. Specifically, the first eigenvector of the principal component of the raw fluorescence data is identified as synchronized dynamics and is projected out from the recordings.

Both the simple discretization and more elaborate OOPSI package (Vogelstein et al. 2010) were used to infer the spike trains from the Calcium waves. Signals with and without deflation of the synchronized dynamics were all discretized using the above two schemes. For the OOPSI scheme, we used the fast_oopsi implementation to speed up the preprocessing. The iteration runs were set to 5–8 depending on the SNR of the data. After filtering with OOPSI, the 1% largest non-zero entries were identified as spiking time points while the rest were identified as noise and discarded.

We also separated the individual responses during synchronized bursting. We first identified the spiking time points of the synchronized dynamics using an OOPSI filter. Then the response of individual neurons, during the synchronized bursting period, was characterized as the Calcium imaging intensity increase at the spiking time point.

2.2 Csiszár's Transfer Entropy

In probability theory, a divergence measure is a function $D(P \parallel Q)$ that measures the difference between two probability distributions P and Q. The most widely used divergence measure is the Kullback-Leibler (K-L) divergence, with the mutual information as a special case. This idea was later generalized by Csiszár, which resulted into a family of divergence measures (Csiszár 1963). This is known as the Csiszár's f-divergence, which is defined as

$$D_f(P \parallel Q) \equiv \int_\Omega f\left(\frac{dP}{dQ}\right) dQ.$$

where f is an convex function satisfying $f(1) = 0$.

The transfer entropy (TE) is a non-parametric statistic measuring the amount of directed (time-asymmetric) transfer of information between two random processes

(Schreiber 2000). It could be interpreted as the reduced uncertainty of future X given the present Y, or the K-L divergence of the transition probability with or without the knowledge of Y. Replacing the log function in TE with the convex function f in the Csiszár's f-divergence, we obtain the more general Csiszár's Transfer Entropy by analogy:

$$\text{CTE}_{Y \to X} = \int_\Omega f\left(\frac{dP(X_{t+1}|X_t^{(k)})}{dP(X_{t+1}|X_t^{(k)}, Y_t^{(k)}, Y_{t+1})}\right) dP(X_{t+1}, X_t^{(k)}, Y_t^{(k)}, Y_{t+1}).$$

Here each $Z_t^{(k)}$ denotes the delay-embedded state vector $(Z_t, \ldots, Z_{t-k+1})$, and the additional Y_{t+1} in the conditioning conforms to the GTE used in Stetter et al. (2012). Binary valued spike trains were used to calculated CTE/GTE. In this study, we use the α-divergence (Liese and Vajda 2006) specified by

$$f(t) = \begin{cases} \frac{4}{1-\alpha^2}\left[1 - t^{(1+\alpha)/2}\right], & \text{if } \alpha \neq \pm 1, \\ t \ln t, & \text{if } \alpha = 1, \\ -\ln t, & \text{if } \alpha = -1. \end{cases}$$

As the K-L divergence is a special case of the *alpha*-divergence, so their performance could be directly compared. Here, the ideal value of α should maximize the AUC score in the training sample. In this studied we discretized the data into binary code indicating whether the neuron is firing, thus making it comparable to GTE. We note more refined binning of the neuron's firing intensity will improve the performance at the cost of larger memory usage. Some other convex functions have also been tested and produce similar best performances (data not shown).

2.3 Correlation Metrics

The conventional Pearson's correlation was also calculated to generate the pooled statistics for optimal connectivity reconstruction as it could be obtained cheaply and proved to be a quite good metric score when the data is properly preprocessed. Specifically, we used the correlation and delayed correlation (with lag 1). The correlation metrics were calculated from the following input data: individual response during the synchronized bursting period, OOPSI-filtered spikes during unsynchronized bursting period. The spikes used to calculate the correlation metrics are real valued to reflect the spiking intensity during bursting and it is more informative compared to correlation calculated from binary valued spike trains. We also tested the performance of more general but computationally more intensive nonlinear kernel-based correlation metric (Bach and Jordan 2003) after the challenge and is briefly discussed in **Supplementary Information**.

2.4 Pooling of Different Metric Scores

Two simple approaches were used to integrate the evidence from different metrics and different preprocessing schemes using the training data. Specifically, we considered the Bayesian posterior probability and a linear combination of metrics. First, the original score obtained from different metric or preprocessing schemes are normalized to the interval [0, 1] according to their ranks. Then the Bayesian posterior probability for the corresponding link being true, given the observed (normalized) metric score $R_{X \to Y}^{data}$, is calculated by

$$P(S_{X \to Y} = 1 | R_{X \to Y}^{data}) = \frac{P(S_{X \to Y} = 1, R_{X \to Y}^{train} = R_{X \to Y}^{data})}{P(R_{X \to Y}^{train} = R_{X \to Y}^{data})}$$

where $S_{X \to Y}$ represents whether there is a true link from X to Y and $R_{X \to Y}$ is a vector of normalized scores. The probability in the above formula could be estimated either by kernel smoothing or binning. To ensure sufficient samples for estimating the probability, we restricted the dimension of $R_{X \to Y}$ to two. We also use the following simple linear combination to aggregate the evidence from two different metrics $\tilde{R}$ and $\hat{R}$:

$$R_{X \to Y}^{joint} = \omega \tilde{R}_{X \to Y}^{data} + (1 - \omega)\hat{R}_{X \to Y}^{data},$$
$$\text{where } \omega = \arg\max_{\omega} \text{AUC}(\omega \tilde{R}_{X \to Y}^{train} + (1 - \omega)\hat{R}_{X \to Y}^{train}).$$

These two approaches defining the basic hybridization operation on the pool of all metric scores. Enlightened by staked ensemble learners (Zhou 2012), we adopted an evolutionary-like hybridization procedure that heuristically mates two relevant[1] or best performing metric scores and then adds their best offspring to the pool. We then repeated this procedure until the best AUC score in the pool no longer increased.

2.5 Regularization on the Recovered Network

We observe that for all the metrics scores we obtained, the degree distribution of the reconstructed networks differs from the genuine wiring that generated the data. The presynaptic and postsynaptic links of the estimated hub nodes are often overestimated while some of the non-hub nodes are disconnected from the estimated network. In this light we argue that in order to obtain more realistic reconstruction, we must regularize the network topology - to some extent. In this study, we did this by explicitly reweighting the score metrics to suppress the links related to the hub nodes and to encourage the links that wire the disconnected nodes back to the network. The reweighting procedure is outlined in Algorithm 1 in **Supplementary Information**.

---

[1]Relevant in the sense that they are derived from same input data or same metric score.

2.6 *Evaluation of the Reconstruction Performance*

The network reconstruction was considered as a binary classification problem. The solution returns a numerical score for each directed neuron pair indicating the confidence that there is a directed connection, with higher values indicating a more likely connection. The results of the classification, obtained by thresholding the prediction score, may be represented in a confusion matrix, where **tp** (true positive), **fn** (false negative), **tn** (true negative) and **fp** (false positive) represent the number of examples falling into each possible outcome. The sensitivity (also called true positive rate or hit rate) and the specificity (true negative rate) as:

True positive ratio = tp/pos
False positive ratio = fp/neg

Here **pos = tp + fp, neg = tn + fn** indicating the total number of connected and unconnected pairs. The prediction results are evaluated with the AUC, which corresponds to the area under the curve obtained by plotting the "True positive ratio" against the "False positive ratio" by varying a threshold on the prediction values to determine the classification result.

3   Results

In this section, we present an empirical study of our proposed procedure on the four training sets (**normal**-1 $\sim$ 4) provided in Connectomics Challenge. Each of these training sets is comprised of approximately 170,000 continuous recordings sampled at 50 Hz of 1,000 neurons with 1.2% connected pairs. Interested readers may refer to Stetter et al. (2012) for details of the simulation setup.

3.1 *CTE*

We compared the performance of the CTE with the GTE. A family of the CTE was obtained by varying the parameter α and the resulting α-AUC curves are shown in Fig. 1. For the 4 datasets, the peak of the α-AUC curves consistently appeared around $\alpha \approx 4$. And the differential sensitivity with respect to the dynamical regime is surprising. While the CTE only offers small advantage in the non-synchronized bursting regime ($\sim 4 \times 10^{-3}$), it significantly improved the reconstruction in the synchronized bursting regime ($\sim 9 \times 10^{-2}$ in this illustration, and even more drastically using some other discretization scheme). It is interesting to notice that the AUC score of the traditional K-L Transfer Entropy happens to fall on the bottom of the valley in the synchronized regime.

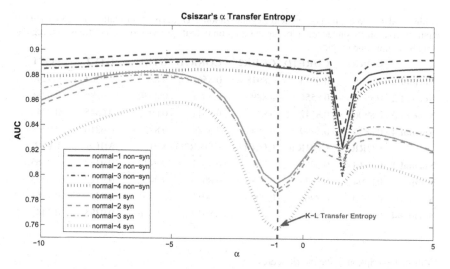

Fig. 1 The AUC score of Csiszár's transfer entropy with different values of the parameter α. *Blue* curves are obtained from the non-synchronized regime while the *green* curves from the synchronized regime. The intersections with the red curve correspond to the traditional K-L GTE (color figure online)

3.2 Pooling Metrics Scores

The effectiveness of pooling different metric scores is presented in Table 1. In the upper panel of the table AUC scores of a representative subset of the the raw metric scores used along with their pooled metric score (using all the raw metric scores) are tabulated for the 4 validation datasets. The tuning parameters are optimized for dataset 'normal-3' and used by the rest of datasets. As shown, pooling significantly boosts the performance of the reconstruction evaluated by AUC scores. The fifth column of lower panel of the table gives one of the best (and fastest) winning solutions based on inverse correlation,[2] and combining it with our best solution (column **POOL**) gives extra $4 \sim 6 \times 10^{-3}$ boost in AUC score (column **BEST**), which beats all best solutions during the contest. Detailed description of those metric scores and whether they are used in the challenge could be find in Table 2.

3.3 Network Regularization

The gain using network regularization is presented in the lower panel of Table 1. The column name indicates the regularization used. For the raw metric score **CORR2**

---

[2]http://www.kaggle.com/c/connectomics/forums/t/8186/fast-matlab-code-to-get-a-score-of-93985.

Table 1 AUC Score with Pooling and Regularization. † D: delayed correlation, i: regularizing on input (postsynaptic connections), o: regularizing on output (presynaptic connections), io: regularizing both input and output)

	CORR1	CORR1D	CORR2	CORR2D	GTE1	GTE2	POOL
Normal-1	0.8888	0.8585	0.8918	0.5568	0.8892	0.6503	0.9240
Normal-2	0.8934	0.8556	0.8894	0.5328	0.8930	0.6289	0.9256
Normal-3	0.8906	0.8542	0.8920	0.5611	0.8932	0.6545	0.9248
Normal-4	0.8876	0.8499	0.8844	0.5380	0.8721	0.6216	0.9217
	CORR2	CORR2i	CORR2o	CORR2io	MIC	MICo	BEST
Normal-1	0.8918	0.8955	0.8997	0.9001	0.9412	0.9422	0.9465
Normal-2	0.8894	0.8938	0.8986	0.8991	0.9412	0.9422	0.9473
Normal-3	0.8920	0.8966	0.9009	0.9015	0.9394	0.9405	0.9461
Normal-4	0.8844	0.8883	0.8928	0.8934	0.9376	0.9385	0.9441

Table 2 Description of the metric scores

	CORR1	CORR2	GTE1	GTE2	POOL	BEST
Individual response (syn)	O	–	–	–	–	–
OOPSI-filtered (non-syn)	–	O	–	–	–	–
Discretization (syn)	–	–	O	–	–	–
Discretization (non-syn)	–	–	–	O	–	–
Use entire sequence	–	–	–	–	–	O
Binary	–	–	O	O	–	–
Used in challenge	O	O	O	O	O	–
Challenge submission	–	–	–	–	O	–

this could bring up the AUC score by about 1×10^{-2}. For the inverse correlation metric it can still elevate the AUC score by 1×10^{-3}. We noticed that regularizing the output links resulted in larger gain compared with regularizing the input links. We note that our regularization scheme is definitely not a universal fix as it certainly depends on the assumption that the distribution of training data and testing data is the same, and violation of this assumption will lead to deteriorated performance.

3.4 Challenge Results

The final performance of our challenge solution and post-challenge solution in the 2014 Connectomics Challenge is presented in Table 3 together with the winner's performance. Our best post-challenge solution outperform the best challenge solution by a large margin.

Table 3 Results table

Team name	Killertom
Final private leaderboard performance	0.93011 (ranking 9th)
Winner's performance	0.94161 (team **AAAGV**)
Our post-challenge best performance	**0.94663** (**BEST** in Table 1)

4 Discussion

Our method is based on linear combination of correlation coefficient and CTE, using data preprocessed with simple discretization, OPPSI filter and PCA. Most of the winning teams' solutions relied on correlation-based metrics, and inverse correlation in particular. Some teams used more sophisticated machine learning tools such as deep CNN, random forest, SVM, etc. Some participants also came up with certain network regularization schemes such as network deconvolution or directly including node-wise relative metric score into the model. Most teams emphasized the paramount importance of preprocessing the noisy calcium imaging data. Our approach seems to be the only one which still extensively uses entropy-based statistics among all the winning parties, possibly due to the costly computational burden involved. We resolve this by optimizing the MATLAB subroutine provided by the organizer which ended up running 20 times faster on desktop than the C++ implementation also provided by the organizer on cluster. As shown in column **BEST** in Table 1, there is still much room for improvement by combining our approach with other winning teams' solutions, even if their AUC score is 1×10^{-2} better than our results.

One significant problem that applies to most of the winning team approaches, including ours, is that the optimal predictability for connectivity is 'learnt from training samples' rather than 'inferred from the dynamics observed', as in reality it is infeasible to obtain real training samples and simulation based surrogates might be biased. We argue that it is the dynamical properties that matter, and instead of statistical solutions, we should start looking for apparatus from the theory of dynamical systems (Sugihara et al. 2012). Also, most participants are still determining the causal links in a pair-wise fashion, with the possibility of gaining information from a more holistic perspective is left uncharted. Those computationally feasible nonlinear association measures (Gretton et al. 2008) might serve as substitutes for those computationally demanding entropy-based statistics.

Acknowledgements First, we thank the challenge organizers for their hard work setting up such an excellent challenge. We also would like to thank Prof. David Waxman and Dr. Wenbo Sheng for the fruitful discussions. C Tao is supported by China Scholarship Council. W Lin is supported by NNSF of China (Grant Nos. 11322111 and 61273014), and from Talents Programs (Nos. 10SG02 and NCET-11-0109). J Feng is s a Royal Society Wolfson Research Merit Award holder, partially supported by National Centre for Mathematics and Interdisciplinary Sciences (NCMIS) in Chinese Academy of Sciences.

Appendix A. Supplementary Information

Algorithm 1: Regularizing the network via reweighing

---

1. Sort the neurons according to their largest in(out) score
   $RC_{i,\cdot}$: the column corresponding to i^{th} largest in $\{\max(C_{k,\cdot})\}$
2. Reweigh the first K in(out) links for each neuron via
   $RC_{i,j}^{v_1} = (1 + \alpha \frac{j}{n})RC_{i,j}$
3. Calculate the probability of the in(out) links of the ith-ranking neuron being connected
   given the training data (sorted in the same fashion)
   $PS_{i,\cdot} = \underset{|k-i|<B}{\text{average}}(RS_{k,\cdot}^{train})$
4. Smooth individual neuron's PS score
   $PS_{i,\cdot}^{sm} = \text{smooth}(PS_{i,\cdot})$
5. Prioritizing the entries with PS^{sm} exceeding the threshold γ while taking the current
   estimate of connectivity strength into consideration
   $RC_{i,j}^{v_2} = \chi_{[PS_{i,j}^{sm}>\gamma]}(1 + PS_{i,j}^{sm} + \beta RC_{i,j}^{v_1}) + \chi_{[PS_{i,j}^{sm}\leq\gamma]}RC_{i,j}^{v_1}$
6. Enforcing a minimum number of L in(out) links for each neuron
   $RC_{i,j}^{v_3} = \chi_{[j<l]} + RC_{i,j}^{v_2}$

The set of tuning parameters $\{K, L, B, \alpha, \beta, \gamma\}$ are selected to maximize AUC score in the training data.

Appendix B. Kernel-Based Correlation Metric

We used the generalized-variance in Jordan's ICA paper to characterize the nonlinear kernel correlation. Specifically, only the first eigenvalue is used. The kernel-based correlation gives similar performance in instantaneous coupling (Pearson $0.888 \approx 0.896$ vs. kernel $0.889 \approx 0.896$) while it significantly outperforms Pearson's correlation in lag-1 correlation (Pearson $0.550 \approx 0.564$ vs. kernel $0.706 \approx 0.711$). This is because the lag-1 dynamics exhibits a highly nonlinear pattern. More detailed results and discussion will be presented in a separate paper.

References

Francis R Bach and Michael I Jordan. Kernel independent component analysis. *The Journal of Machine Learning Research*, 3:1–48, 2003.
I. Csiszár. Eine informationstheoretische Ungleichung und ihre Anwendung auf den Beweis der Ergodizitat von Markoffschen Ketten. *Publ. Math. Inst. Hungar. Acad*, 8:85–108, 1963.
Arthur Gretton, Kenji Fukumizu, Choon Hui Teo, Le Song, Bernhard Schölkopf, and Alex J Smola. A kernel statistical test of independence. 2008.

Christine Grienberger and Arthur Konnerth. Imaging calcium in neurons. *Neuron*, 73(5):862–885, 2012.

Friedrich Liese and Igor Vajda. On divergences and informations in statistics and information theory. *Information Theory, IEEE Transactions on*, 52(10):4394–4412, 2006.

Thomas Schreiber. Measuring information transfer. *Physical review letters*, 85(2):461, 2000.

Olav Stetter, Demian Battaglia, Jordi Soriano, and Theo Geisel. Model-free reconstruction of excitatory neuronal connectivity from calcium imaging signals. *PLoS computational biology*, 8(8):e1002653, 2012.

George Sugihara, Robert May, Hao Ye, Chih-hao Hsieh, Ethan Deyle, Michael Fogarty, and Stephan Munch. Detecting causality in complex ecosystems. *science*, 338(6106):496–500, 2012.

Joshua T Vogelstein, Adam M Packer, Timothy A Machado, Tanya Sippy, Baktash Babadi, Rafael Yuste, and Liam Paninski. Fast nonnegative deconvolution for spike train inference from population calcium imaging. *Journal of neurophysiology*, 104(6):3691–3704, 2010.

Zhi-Hua Zhou. *Ensemble methods: foundations and algorithms*. CRC Press, 2012.

Neural Connectivity Reconstruction from Calcium Imaging Signal Using Random Forest with Topological Features

Wojciech M. Czarnecki and Rafal Jozefowicz

*Editors: Demian Battaglia, Isabelle Guyon, Vincent Lemaire,
Javier Orlandi, Bisakha Ray, Jordi Soriano*

Abstract Connectomics is becoming an increasingly popular area of research. With the recent advances in optical imaging of the neural activity tens of thousands of neurons can be monitored simultaneously. In this paper we present a method of incorporating topological knowledge inside data representation for Random Forest classifier in order to reconstruct the neural connections from patterns of their activities. Proposed technique leads to the model competitive with state-of-the art methods like Deep Convolutional Neural Networks and Graph Decomposition techniques. This claim is supported by the results (5th place with 0.003 in terms of AUC ROC loss to the top contestant) obtained in the connectomics competition organized on the Kaggle platform.

Keywords Random forest · Neural connectivity reconstruction · Connectome · Topological features

The original form of this article appears in JMLR W&CP Volume 46.

W.M. Czarnecki (✉)
Faculty of Mathematics and Computer Science, Jagiellonian University, Krakow, Poland
e-mail: wojciech.czarnecki@uj.edu.pl

R. Jozefowicz
Google Inc., New York, NY, USA
e-mail: rafalj@google.com

1 Introduction

The study of connectomes is becoming an increasingly popular area of research.
With the recent advances in optical imaging of the neural activity tens of thousands of
neurons can be monitored simultaneously. We are trying to solve an inverse problem:
reconstruct the original direct connections between neurons based on their patterns
of activities.

Many tools have been proposed for the neural connectivity reconstruction based on
their time series activity. Used approaches range from simple coefficients computed
for each pair of signals, like Transfer Entropy (TE) (Honey et al. 2007) and its further
modification – Generalized Transfer Entropy (GTE) (Stetter et al. 2012) to machine
learning approaches designed specifically for this kind of problem, like Friedman
et al. Graphical Lasso model (Friedman et al. 2008). The proposed method exploits
multiple causality indices to reconstruct the graph with use of the topological features
to indirectly achieve the similar task to Graphical Lasso. Instead of modifying or
developing a new method, we show how one can manipulate the data representation
to make it possible to achieve good results with use of a standard classification method
– Random Forest (Breiman 2001).

The rest of the paper is structured as follows. Section 2 describes in detail the
methods used by the proposed approach. In Sect. 3 we show the methodology used
for testing the experiments and the comparison of the results. Finally, in Sect. 4 we
summarize our findings and the properties of the proposed solution.

2 Methods

In the proposed approach, we deal with the neural connectivity reconstruction from
the neurons' activity time series by modeling it as a simple binary classification
problem. Each pair of neurons is represented by a constant size real vector, where
each dimension is one feature value. In other words, given time series of i'th neuron
x_i we create a point

$$p_{ij} = [f_1(x_i, x_j), f_2(x_i, x_j), \ldots, f_n(x_i, x_j)]^T \in \mathbb{R}^n,$$

such that each f_k is one feature extractor. For simplicity we use the notation
$f_k(i, j) := f_k(x_i, x_j)$. Our training set consists of pairs (p_{ij}, c_{ij}) where c_{ij} equals 1
if there is a directed edge between i'th and j'th neuron, and 0 otherwise.

We have chosen Random Forest (RF) (Breiman 2001) as the underlying classification tool due to its high efficiency and parallelism. We are dealing with the
classification problem, where training set consists of millions of points in the input
space with more than a hundred dimensions. Training other non-linear models (like
kernelized SVMs, or even KNN) take significantly more time. Unfortunately, there
are some limitations, which make application of this model difficult for a considered

problem. Most importantly, RF in its basic, most efficient implementation, is unable to use any combination of features to make a decision. As a result, it is sensitive to relations as simple as linear combinations of the dimensions. For example, adding $f_i - f_j$ can significantly improve the classification process. This also explains our focus on adding various feature transformations to the input space that would help the classifier make better decisions. We evaluated many of them and will go into more detail about the process in the later subsections.

There are two basic types of features extractors used:

- we use existing, well known features including correlation coefficient or generalized transfer entropy,
- we introduce topological features, which encode the various graph's structure information in our representation.

Now we briefly describe both types of features.

2.1 Efficient Features Extraction

The dataset for a single network consists of a time series of neural activities for each of the 1000 neurons. The data itself is simulated but should closely resemble real recordings of cultured neurons. This allows us to have ground truth of connections, which is desirable for evaluation purposes. We are given a one hour of recording with 50 Hz frequency (approximately 180,000 data points per neuron) and the goal of the problem is to determine, for each pair of neurons, whether there is a direct connection between them.

It is worth noting that, in our problem, the average length of neuron's spike is shorter than the available frame rate of captured activities. This is a property of the simulator to model the limited time resolution and not allowing to easily separate individual spikes. Because of that, we can safely assume that if the inferred spikes occur more than 2 frames away, they can be considered independent (not directly influenced).

A simple pre-processing scheme was applied to the raw data in order to retrieve spike times of the neurons. We looked at the series of the differences of the two consecutive elements and put them into 2 or 3 buckets (which gave us one level of parameterization) based on the chosen quantiles from overall network data. Furthermore, as suggested in Stetter et al. (2012), we filtered out the points in time in which the mean neural activity exceeded the chosen threshold.

We have used several different base predictors that were computed on each pair of the neural activities (pre-processed):

- Cross-correlation (XC), $E[(X - \overline{X})(Y - \overline{Y})]$.
- Cross-correlation with a lag of 1 frame (XC-L1).
- Generalized Transfer Entropy (GTE), $H(Y^t | Y^{t-1}, Y^{t-2}) - H(Y^t | Y^{t-2}, Y^{t-1}, X^{t-1}, X^t)$, where $H(X)$ is a Shannon entropy of X.

- Information Gain, $G(Y^t|Y^{t-1}) - G(Y^t|X^t, Y^{t-1})$, where $G(X)$ is a Gini index (IGG) or a Shannon entropy of X (IGE).

One notable property of the above metrics is that we compare the values of the two series at the same point time (Instant Feedback Term - IFT) with the exception of XC-L1. This is important with the limited resolution of the raw data as the neurons often appear to spike at the same time on the recording. IFT allows us to capture this information.

With the 5 base algorithms, we considered 2 ways of splitting the raw data into buckets and 12 different mean activity thresholds. We used all 120 possible combinations as features for RF and let the learning algorithm find the best parameters.

Since this is a computationally intensive task we have developed efficient implementations of the algorithms in Python with the critical paths written in Cython. A single method requires 600 MB of RAM and about 20 min of a single CPU time using modern hardware, which is orders of magnitude faster than the computation times mentioned in Stetter et al. (2012). Furthermore, because of its low memory footprint, the approach easily scales linearly with the number of available CPU cores. This allowed us to iterate quickly and evaluate many potential features.

It is also worth mentioning that we have tried many other candidates as base predictors, including lagged and weighted correlations, Granger causality and GTE on the reversed time series. We did not notice any significant improvements when using them along with the chosen features and realized that adding more feature transformations gives us much higher impact.

Table 1 summarizes the performance of the base predictors. The information gain metric with Gini index turns out to be used the most in the final model. One explanation of the poor performance of XC-L1 is the fact that it's missing the information about the spikes that appear to occur at the same time (by the definition of the metric). As for GTE, it might be the case that it's looking at the values too far out in the past (depends on the values of three consecutive frames at any given point), which is adding more noise to the predictor. It could have been more successful if the frame rate was higher. The other explanation could be that, as noted in Stetter et al. (2012), with the optimal conditioning level IGE/IGG can out-perform GTE. Random Forest might be doing a good job in deciding which threshold is the best for a given network resulting in the superior results of the information gain methods.

Table 1 Analysis of the base features in the final model. TOPX denotes how many features in top X most important features were using the particular base predictor

Base feature	Importance	TOP10	TOP50	TOP100
IGG	0.62	9	26	51
IGE	0.18	1	9	27
XC	0.15	0	15	20
XC-L1	0.04	0	0	1
GTE	0.01	0	0	1

2.2　Random Forest

Random Forest (Breiman 2001) (RF) is a very successful ensemble learning technique for both classification and regression problems using decision (or regression) trees. The main idea behind this algorithm is to perform a bagging (bootstrap aggregation) together with a random subspaces method. Given a constant B (size of the forest), the tree bagging performs the following steps:

1. for $k = 1$ to B

   (a) sample with replacement N training samples from $T = \{(p_{ij}, c_{ij})\}_{i,j}^{N}$ to create T_i.
   (b) train a decision tree on T_i and call the resulting predictor $t_k : \mathbb{R}^n \to \{0, 1\}$.

2. return predictor

$$t(p) = \arg \max_{c \in \{0,1\}} v(c, p),$$

where $v(c, p) = |\{t_k(p) = c : k \in \{1, \ldots, B\}\}|$.

The only modification that is used in Random Forest is to train a non-classical decision tree in step 1. (b), namely, at each node split the random subset of features is selected to be considered. This small modification adds an important regularization to the whole training process, so the valid choice of the size of this random subset is crucial. For classification procedure a well known heuristic is to chose a number of features equal to the square root of the input space. In our solution we tuned this parameter in order to find the most appropriate size of the random subspaces and found out that in this particular problem the optimal value is a bit bigger (40).

The choice of such classifier was mainly motivated by:

- its highly parallel structure – each t_k can be independently trained and evaluated,
- fast training time as the decision trees are very simple classifiers,
- existence of efficient, free implementations like the one in SCIKIT- LEARN Pedregosa et al. (2011),
- giving a direct estimation of the classification confidence $\hat{P}(c|p) = v(c, p)/B$.
- dealing well with missing features (not the case in our scenario, but could be helpful in general as some statistics may be undefined in border cases).

Unfortunately, RFs have some drawbacks, namely:

- they consist of many metaparameters that have to be tuned,
- they are unable to express any, even linear, combinations of features in general (some modifications, like Rotation Forests (Rodriguez et al. 2006) have been proposed but they are much less efficient).

Both of these problems are solved (to some extent) by introduction of the specific topological features and a heuristic method of training described in the further sections.

2.3 Random Forest with Topological Features

The true input data has a graphical form, which means that there are important relations encoded in the mutual location of particular neurons. For example, for the exact causality detection it is not only important how high are some causality-related features between i'th and j'th neuron, but also what are the same features computed in the opposite direction. This leads to the need of incorporating features into the data representation, which include graph structure and can be directly used by the RF. During heavy testing we have developed the set of topological features, which significantly increase the model's quality.

For each particular feature extractor f (being for example GTE with threshold 0.12) we considered:

- Normalized difference $\frac{f(i,j)-f(j,i)}{f(i,j)+f(j,i)}$, in order to detect the edge's direction it is important to know whether the opposite direction is more or less likely. The normalization helps to work with wide range of possible $f(i,j)$ values in a uniform way.
- Geometrical closure $\max_k \sqrt{f(i,k)f(k,j)}$, in order to check whether the high "causality" between i'th and j'th neuron is a result of an existence of k'th neuron, through which the signal actually flows.
- Markov closure $\sum_k f(i,k)f(k,j)$, assuming that we view the whole problem as a kind of Markov process, where states are describing which neuron spikes, we can compute the overall probability of going from i'th neuron spike to j'th neuron spike, if $f(i,j)$ is a transition probability.
- Feature ratios $\frac{f(i,j)}{\max_k f(k,j)}$, $\frac{f(i,j)}{\max_k f(i,k)}$, $\frac{f(i,j)}{\max_k f(i,k)f(k,j)}$, $\frac{f(i,j)}{\sum_k f(i,k)f(k,j)}$ which were included due to the limitations of the RF model that was unable to divide two existing features by themselves.
- Scaled ratios $\frac{f(i,j)}{\sqrt{\sum_k f(i,k)f(k,j)}}$, $\frac{f(i,j)}{(\sum_k (f(i,k)f(k,j))^{3/2})^{1/3}}$, $\frac{f(i,j)}{\max_k \sqrt{f(i,k)f(k,j)}}$ to neglect some scale issues.
- Network Deconvolution: $F \cdot (I + F)^{-1}$ inspired by Feizi et al. (2013), where F is a matrix such that $F_{ij} = f(i,j)$. If we treat F as a transitive closure of some matrix G such that $\lim_{n\to\infty} G^n = 0$ (with some additional assumptions), then the given formula is an inverse operation to $F = G + G^2 + \cdots = G \cdot (I - G)^{-1}$. The intuition behind is that, in some sense, G captures the direct relationships between the neurons.

It is worth noting, that each such topological feature adds as many new dimensions, as there are non-topological features[1] in the representation. So, for example, if we have 4 types of features extractors, each with 6 types of some parameters (thresholds), then each topological feature actually adds $4 \times 6 = 24$ new dimensions. However, adding all of such features would significantly increase the input space size and lead

---

[1]Except normalized difference which is also applied for all non-symmetrical topological and non-topological features.

to the weaker classifier due to the *curse of dimensionality*. Luckily, RF can be used in a greedy, closed loop manner, which enables us to iteratively change the data representation.

2.4 Random Forest Training with Constant Representation Changes

In order to deal with the increasing number of dimensions as well as the fact, that model's metaparameters (number of minimum samples in a leaf, maximum number of features considered, etc.) heavily depend on the input space dimensionality we propose the following closed loop process for each new topological features f' to be considered and for a representation ϕ with a model currently scoring s_ϕ under some metric (like in our case AUC ROC score).

1. take next f',
2. add f' to current representation ϕ forming $\phi_{f'}^+$,
3. train forest on the whole dataset using $\phi_{f'}^+$.,
4. Compute the *relative feature importances* (averaged expected fraction of the samples features contribute to) for each $f \in \phi_{f'}^+$ and drop as many worst dimensions, as there were added by f' forming $\phi_{f'}$,
5. evaluate forest using leave-one-out cross validation using $\phi_{f'}$ getting score $s_{\phi_{f'}}$,
6. if $s_{\phi_{f'}} > s_\phi$ then $\phi \leftarrow \phi_{f'}, s_\phi \leftarrow s_{\phi_{f'}}$,
7. goto 1.

It is easy to see that such procedure ensures constant size representation, which reduces the problem of the high dimensionality and the requirement of constant metaparameters refitting.

Table 2 summarizes the results of the proposed methodology by providing final importance of each topological feature in our Random Forest. One interesting phenomenon is a very high usage of the Minkovsky-like scaling of the Markov closure based ratio. This may be a result of the minor scaling issues (each network has a bit different values, this Minkovsky scaling makes the differences much less significant).

3 Evaluation

The proposed method was evaluated during the CONNECTOMICS[2] competition organized by CHALLENGES IN MACHINE LEARNING[3] and hosted on the Kaggle[4] platform. The duration of the contest was 3 months in which the participants were

---

[2]http://www.kaggle.com/c/connectomics/.

[3]http://www.chalearn.org/.

[4]http://www.kaggle.com.

Table 2 Analysis of the features in the final model. TOPX denotes how many features in top X most important features were using the particular topology out of the total 535 best features chosen in the procedure described earlier

Topological feature	Equation	Importance	TOP10	TOP50	TOP100
No topology	$f(i, j)$	0.01	0	0	0
Normalized difference	$\frac{f(i,j)-f(j,i)}{f(i,j)+f(j,i)}$	0.06	0	0	4
Geometrical closure	$\max_k \sqrt{f(i, k)f(k, j)}$	0.09	0	4	16
Markov closure	$\sum_k f(i, k)f(k, j)$	0.05	0	1	18
Feature ratios 1	$\frac{f(i,j)}{\max_k f(k,j)}$	0.01	0	0	1
Feature ratios 2	$\frac{f(i,j)}{\max_k f(i,k)}$	0.15	1	5	14
Feature ratios 3	$\frac{f(i,j)}{\max_k f(i,k)f(k,j)}$	0.03	0	0	6
Feature ratios 4	$\frac{f(i,j)}{\sum_k f(i,k)f(k,j)}$	0.04	0	1	18
Scaled ratios 1	$\frac{f(i,j)}{\sqrt{\sum_k f(i,k)f(k,j)}}$	0.23	3	14	18
Scaled ratios 2	$\frac{f(i,j)}{(\sum_k (f(i,k)f(k,j))^{3/2})^{1/3}}$	0.46	6	26	33
Scaled ratios 3	$\frac{f(i,j)}{\max_k \sqrt{f(i,k)f(k,j)}}$	0.05	0	4	10

required to submit solutions in the csv format for the 2 networks. The submitted file should consist of one real number for each pair (ordered) of neurons of the two held out networks, representing the confidence of whether there is a directed connection between the given nodes. After each submission, the participants would receive an instant feedback with the score on one of the held out networks (Valid). To prevent the overfitting the solutions were ranked based on the scores of the second network (Test) and the final results were only available after the competition ended. The metric used for models' evaluation was an area under the ROC curve, which is a standard metric in such tasks (Stetter et al. 2012).

We used code written mainly in Python (with Cython elements) with the use of the NUMPY, SCIPY and SCIKIT- LEARN (Pedregosa et al. 2011) libraries. The tests were performed on the Fermi supercomputer consisting of 64 computational units (eight 8-core processors) to exploit the parallel nature of used model. However, it would be also possible to run the whole solution directly on the GPU units as feature extractors, topological features and RF training itself can be easily done on the GPU unit (Van Essen et al. 2012).

The dataset used for the evaluation purposes consists of a time series of four (1,000 neurons each) networks activity. Additional two networks were held out by organizers, so they were not used during internal evaluation, however, the scores of our final model are available. Due to our approach, this gives 4,000,000 samples of a binary classification problem.

All metaparameters were fitted using leave-one-out cross validation. We considered each network as one "set of samples", and performed LOO on this level of

Table 3 Results of different models under AUC ROC metric for leave-one-out cross validation on 4 networks (LOO), hold-out valid (Valid) and test (Test) networks

Model (team name at Kaggle)	Features	LOO	Valid	Test
Logistic Regression	Basic	0.90245	–	–
SVM	Basic	0.90305	–	–
Random Forest	Basic	0.90910	–	–
Random Forest	+normalized difference	0.91326	0.91977	0.91720
Random Forest	+geometrical closure	0.92635	0.92795	0.92757
Random Forest	+markov closure	0.93062	0.93239	0.93250
Random Forest	+feature ratios	0.93597	0.93618	0.93634
Random Forest (Lejlot and Rafal)	+scaled ratios	0.93781	0.93761	0.93826
Random Forest	+network deconvolution	0.94224	0.94239	**0.94269**
Deep CNN (Lukasz 8000)	Raw signal	–	0.93920	0.93956
Partial Correlations (AAAGV)	–	–	0.94262	0.94161

granularity (so there were 4 iterations, in each we trained on 3,000,000 points and tested on 1,000,000, all coming from never seen before network). The process of adding topological features was performed according to the scheme from the previous section.

Table 3 summarizes the results obtained for the considered models (team Lejlot and Rafal) as well as two competitors' approaches. One of them is a Deep Convolutional Neural Network (Sainath et al. 2013) trained on the pure signal (team Lukasz 8000) and the second one is a Partial Correlation Estimation Model based on De La Fuente et al. (2004) (team AAAGV).

It is worth noting that our simple, RF based approach, where the model is not well suited neither for the time series processing nor for the graph reconstruction, behaves very well. In particular, it achieves about $0.001 - 0.002$ worse results than a deep neural network, being at the same time much simpler model and implemented in dozens of existing libraries. On the other hand it achieves score around 0.003 (result on the Valid set seems to be overfitting due to the great decrease in the result on the test network) from the partial correlations model.

Our cross-validation scheme estimates the score on hold-out networks really well, suggesting that this RF solution is not overfitting the training data. It was interesting to see that while we were adding more features, the LOO estimations were getting closer to the scores on the unseen networks (as can be observed from the table).

It seems to be another proof of wide applicability of Random Forest model, which after adding topological features is able to compete head-to-head with state-of-the-art methods.

The proposed method achieved 5th place in the competition (losing about 0.003 in terms of AUC ROC). However, among all best scoring teams, only the proposed approach was using different model from Partial Correlations, Network Deconvolution and Deep Convolutional Neural Network.

After the competition ended, we analyzed the performance of a simplified version of the Network Deconvolution algorithm for a feature extractor, as suggested by one of the contestants. It improved our solution further and beating the top result from the competition by approximately 0.001.

4   Conclusions

To the best of our knowledge using a binary classifier with topological features is a different approach than taken by other competitors and to what we could find in the existing literature. It has also some interesting properties:

- The feature generation and training/prediction of the Random Forest algorithm is fully parallelizable and it scales linearly with the number available of processors (up to the point of training one tree, which is on the order of minutes).
- The prediction for the edge between nodes i and j depends only on the metrics for neighbors of i and j. Due to its local nature it has potential to be applicable for much larger graphs since we are not required to keep the whole graph in memory. We just need to be able to compute metrics for the neurons that are close enough to i and j.
- It makes very little assumptions about the underlying neurobiological setting of the problem and it is based only on the simple characteristics of the data (like correlations of neural activities). In fact, the only part that is related to neuron activities is the simple initial filtering and pre-processing. The model behaves very well even though the spike inference is very basic and far from perfect. It is also easy to explain and implement.
- The method does not assume the graph to be undirected as opposed to graphical lasso approach and thus can extract directed relationships between neurons.

References

Leo Breiman. Random forests. *Machine learning*, 45 (1): 5–32, 2001.
Alberto De La Fuente, Nan Bing, Ina Hoeschele, and Pedro Mendes. Discovery of meaningful associations in genomic data using partial correlation coefficients. *Bioinformatics*, 20 (18): 3565–3574, 2004.
Soheil Feizi, Daniel Marbach, Muriel Médard, and Manolis Kellis. Network deconvolution as a general method to distinguish direct dependencies in networks. *Nature biotechnology*, 2013.
Jerome Friedman, Trevor Hastie, and Robert Tibshirani. Sparse inverse covariance estimation with the graphical lasso. *Biostatistics*, 9 (3): 432–441, 2008.
Christopher J Honey, Rolf Kötter, Michael Breakspear, and Olaf Sporns. Network structure of cerebral cortex shapes functional connectivity on multiple time scales. *Proceedings of the National Academy of Sciences*, 104 (24): 10240–10245, 2007.

Fabian Pedregosa, Gaël Varoquaux, Alexandre Gramfort, Vincent Michel, Bertrand Thirion, Olivier Grisel, Mathieu Blondel, Peter Prettenhofer, Ron Weiss, Vincent Dubourg, et al. Scikit-learn: Machine learning in python. *The Journal of Machine Learning Research*, 12: 2825–2830, 2011.

Juan José Rodriguez, Ludmila I Kuncheva, and Carlos J Alonso. Rotation forest: A new classifier ensemble method. *Pattern Analysis and Machine Intelligence, IEEE Transactions on*, 28 (10): 1619–1630, 2006.

Tara N Sainath, Abdel-rahman Mohamed, Brian Kingsbury, and Bhuvana Ramabhadran. Deep convolutional neural networks for lvcsr. In *Acoustics, Speech and Signal Processing (ICASSP), 2013 IEEE International Conference on*, pages 8614–8618. IEEE, 2013.

Olav Stetter, Demian Battaglia, Jordi Soriano, and Theo Geisel. Model-free reconstruction of excitatory neuronal connectivity from calcium imaging signals. *PLoS computational biology*, 8 (8): e1002653, 2012.

Brian Van Essen, Chris Macaraeg, Maya Gokhale, and Ryan Prenger. Accelerating a random forest classifier: Multi-core, gp-gpu, or fpga? In *Field-Programmable Custom Computing Machines (FCCM), 2012 IEEE 20th Annual International Symposium on*, pages 232–239. IEEE, 2012.

Efficient Combination of Pairwise Feature Networks

Pau Bellot and Patrick E. Meyer

Editors: Demian Battaglia, Isabelle Guyon, Vincent Lemaire,
Javier Orlandi, Bisakha Ray, Jordi Soriano

Abstract This paper presents a novel method for the reconstruction of a neural network connectivity using calcium fluorescence data. We introduce a fast unsupervised method to integrate different networks that reconstructs structural connectivity from neuron activity. Our method improves the state-of-the-art reconstruction method General Transfer Entropy (GTE). We are able to better eliminate indirect links, improving therefore the quality of the network via a normalization and ensemble process of GTE and three new informative features. The approach is based on a simple combination of networks, which is remarkably fast. The performance of our approach is benchmarked on simulated time series provided at the connectomics challenge and also submitted at the public competition.

Keywords Network reconstruction algorithms · Elimination of indirect links · Connectomes

The original form of this article appears in JMLR W&CP Volume 46.

P. Bellot (✉)
Department of Signal Theory and Communications, Technical University of Catalonia, UPC-Campus Nord, C/Jordi Girona, 1-3, 08034 Barcelona, Spain
e-mail: pau.bellot@upc.edu

P.E. Meyer
Bioinformatics and Systems Biology (BioSys), Faculty of Sciences, Université de Liège (ULg), 27 Blvd du Rectorat, 4000 Liège, Belgium
e-mail: patrick.meyer@ulg.ac.be
URL: http://www.biosys.ulg.ac.be/

© Springer International Publishing AG 2017
D. Battaglia et al. (eds.), *Neural Connectomics Challenge*, The Springer Series on Challenges in Machine Learning, DOI 10.1007/978-3-319-53070-3_7

1 Introduction

Understanding the general functioning of the brain and its learning capabilities as well as the brain structure and some of its alterations caused by disease, is a key step towards a treatment of epilepsy, Alzheimer's disease and other neuropathologies.

This could be achieved by recovering neural networks from activities. A neural network is a circuit formed by a group of connected (physically or by means of neural signals) neurons that performs a given functionality. These circuits are responsible for reflexes, senses, as well as more complex processes such as learning and memory.

Thanks to fluorescence imaging, we can easily measure the activity of a group of neurons. The changes of fluorescence recorded from the neural tissue are proved to be directly corresponding to neural activity. With calcium imaging one can study the neural activity of a population of neurons simultaneously allowing to uncover the function of neural networks.

But, recovering the exact wiring of the brain (connectome) including nearly 100 billion neurons that have on average 7000 synaptic connections to other neurons is still a daunting task. Hence, there is a growing need for fast and accurate methods able to reconstruct these networks. That is why the ChaLearn non-profit organization has proposed the connectomics challenge. The goal of the competition is to reconstruct the structure of a neural network from temporal patterns of activities of neurons.

2 Typical Methods

There is a wide variety of reconstruction algorithms that are able to infer the network structure from time series. Even though one of the least controversial necessary criterion to establish a cause-effect relationship is temporal precedence, many causal inference algorithms only require conditional independence testing Pearl (2000), or, more recently, joint distribution of pairs of variables Janzing et al. (2010). The work of Clive Granger has lead to a framework that has received a lot of attention due to its simplicity and the successful results Popescu and Guyon (2013).

2.1 Correlation with Discretization

Here, we present a quick review of the simplest method to reconstruct a network, based on the correlation coefficient. The correlation is a standard method to quantify the statistical similarity between two random variables X and Y and it is defined as:

$$corr(X, Y) = \frac{cov(X, Y)}{\sigma_X \sigma_Y} = \frac{E[(X - \mu_X)(Y - \mu_Y)]}{\sigma_X \sigma_Y}, \tag{1}$$

where μ_X and μ_Y are respectively the expected values of X and Y, and σ_X and σ_Y are the standard deviations.

Once we have a correlation coefficient between each pair of neurons, we can construct a co-activity network. If the correlation is greater than a threshold, then the neurons are connected in an undirected way, this strategy is presented at Butte and Kohane (2000), where instead of using the correlation they use Mutual Information which can be seen as a non-linear dependency measure.

2.2 Generalized Transfer Entropy

Here, we present a quick review of one of the state of the art methods, the Transfer Entropy (TE) Schreiber (2000) based measure of effective connectivity called Generalized Transfer Entropy, or GTE Stetter et al. (2012).

The basic idea behind Granger causality to test if the observations of time series of two variables A and B are due to the underlying process "A causes B" rather than "B causes A", is to fit different predictive models A (present time) and B (present time) as a function of A (past times) and B (past times). If A can be better predicted from past values of A than from past values of B, while B is also better predicted by A, then we have an indication for A being the cause of B.

Based on this idea, several methods have been derived in order to improve the results. These methods incorporate the frequency domain analysis instead of a time domain analysis Nolte and Müller (2010). One recent idea is to add contemporaneous values of B to predict A and vice versa to take into account instantaneous causal effect, due for instance to insufficient time resolution Moneta and Spirtes (2005).

Therefore, GTE can be seen as a reconstruction algorithm of causal networks based solely on pairwise interactions.

3 Our Proposal: Unsupervised Ensemble of CLRed Pairwise Features

If A activates B and this last one activates C, is very likely that co-activity networks will find a strong dependency between A and C even though the latter is an indirect link. Gene Network Inference methods have proposed different strategies to eliminate these indirect links Butte and Kohane (2000), Margolin et al. (2006), Meyer et al. (2007).

One of these strategies is the Context Likelihood or Relatedness network (CLR) method Faith et al. (2007). In order to do so, the method derives a score that is associated to the empirical distribution of the score values. Consider a score $S_{i,j}$ indicating the strength of an alleged connection between two neurons i and j. Let us call μ_i and σ_i the mean and standard deviation of this score over all neurons connected to i. The asymmetric standardized score is given as:

$$z_i = max \left(0, \frac{S_{i,j} - \mu_i}{\sigma_i}\right). \tag{2}$$

Finally, the symmetrized score is given by: $z_{ij} = \sqrt{z_i^2 + z_j^2}$. This method has a complexity of $O(n^2)$, n being the number of neurons, and requires a symmetric matrix.

Our unsupervised ensemble of pairwise features uses the CLR algorithm to eliminate indirect links and normalize the network before assembling the different CLRed pairwise features. With the second step we are able to eliminate more indirect links that are still present at one reconstructed network but not at the others. This idea comes from modENCODE Consortium et al. (2010), Marbach et al. (2012), where the authors propose an algorithm to integrate different network inference methods to construct a community networks which is capable of stabilizing the results and recover a good network. Their state-of-the-art method to combine networks is based on rank averaging. The individual ranks of each link are added together to compute the final rank. Then, the final list is computed sorting these score decreasingly. This method is also known as $Ranksum$, and will be referred as RS in the paper.

Instead of this procedure, our proposal that will be referred as $CLRsum$ or CS is formulated as follows:

$$CS := \sum_{i}^{N} CLR(feature_i). \tag{3}$$

A description of the workflow of our network reconstruction process is available in Fig. 1 in the Supplementary Material Bellot and Meyer (2014). In this case, we have used four features that are defined in the following subsections.

3.1   Feature 1: Symmetrized GTE

The first pairwise measure is a modification of the state-of-the-art method GTE (see Sect. 2.2), since we apply the CLR method the recovered network should be undirected. Indeed, the GTE method provides a non-symmetric score ($gte_{i \rightarrow j} \neq gte_{j \rightarrow i}$), we symmetrize it by taking the most conservative score recovered by GTE. This symmetrized GTE network is denoted as GTE_{sym}, and is defined as follows: $gte_{i,j} = min(gte_{i \rightarrow j}, gte_{j \rightarrow i})$.

3.2 Feature 2: Correlation of the Extrema of the Signals

The second pairwise measure is based on the correlation $(corr(X_i, X_j))$ of both signals. But, doing so we are not able to discriminate between true regulations and indirect effects or light scattering effects. We observed experimentally with the provided networks and their respective ground-truth, that the correlation between the signals when one of both neurons is spiking is statistically more informative than the plain correlation.

The quantile $q_{k\%}(x)$ is the data value of x where we have $k\%$ of the values of x above it. The higher the quantile the stronger the statistical correlation between the measure and the connectome network. However, in order to be able to recover a non-spurious correlation at least several hundreds of samples are required. First, we capture the quantile $\alpha\%$ of both signals, and compute the correlation using only the points of both signals that are above the quantile:

$$\text{Let } t_k := X_i(t) \geq q_{\alpha\%}(X_i) \text{ and } t_l := X_j(t) \geq q_{\alpha\%}(X_j)$$
$$ct_{i,j} = corr\left(X_i(t_n), X_j(t_n)\right) \text{ with } t_n := t_k \cup t_l. \tag{4}$$

Computing previous equation between each pair of different neurons we obtain the $CT_{\alpha\%}$ network.

3.3 Feature 3: Mean Squared Error of Difference Signal

The third pairwise feature that we have found experimentally, is complementary to feature 2. Instead of computing the correlation on the spikes, this feature uses the mean squared error of the points where the two signals disagree the most (once both have been normalized by a centering and scaling). The normalization process is defined as $X_i^s := (X_i - \mu_{X_i})/\sigma_{X_i}$.

First, we compute the difference between the two scaled different signals ($i \neq j$) and keep the points where they differ the most. To get such particular time points, we also rely on an small quantile $\alpha\%$:

$$\text{Let } f_{i,j}(t) = X_i^s(t) - X_j^s(t) \text{ and } t_k := d_{i,j}(t) \geq q_{\alpha\%}(f_{i,j})$$
$$\text{Then } X_i' := X_i^s(t_k) \ X_j' := X_j^s(t_k). \tag{5}$$

Once the points of interest (t_k) are extracted, the mean square error between $p_{i,j} := X_i' - X_j'$ and $p_{j,i} := X_j' - X_i'$ is computed. This leads to a non-symmetrical measure. As explained before, CLR requires a symmetric matrix. In order to symmetrize the matrix we take the minimum of $p_{i,j}^2$ and $p_{j,i}^2$ as has been done in feature 1:

$$cd_{i,j} = \min\left((X_i' - X_j')^2, (X_j' - X_i')^2\right).$$

This measure is computed between each pair of different neurons to obtain the $MD_{\alpha\%}$ network.

3.4 Feature 4: Range of Difference Signal

The last pairwise measure that we have found correlated to the connectome is the range of the difference between two neuron signals.

For every pair of neurons we compute the difference between the two different signals ($i \neq j$): $df_{i,j} := X_i - X_j$

Then, the measure captures the range of $df_{i,j}$, but in order to be robust to the presence of noise the range is not the difference between the largest and smallest values of $df_{i,j}$, but the average over the 10th maximal/minimal values of $df_{i,j}$. This measure is computed between each pair of different neurons to obtain the network RD. In order to obtain a similarity network, we invert the network as follows:

$$RD := max(R) - R \text{ with } diag(RD) = 0. \tag{6}$$

4 Experiments

The performance of our algorithm is benchmarked on the data provided at the ChaLearn connectomics challenge. The data reproduces the dynamic behavior of real networks of cultured neurons. The simulator also includes the typical real defects of the calcium fluorescence technology: limited time resolution and light scattering artifacts (the activity of given neuron influences the measurements of nearby neurons) Stetter et al. (2012).

The challenge provides different datasets that have distinct properties, we will use the datasets where the network structure is also provided, i.e., 10 big datasets of 1000 neurons and 5 small datasets of 100 neurons. The network inference problem can be seen as a binary decision problem: after the thresholding of the network provided by the algorithm, the final decision can be seen as a classification: for each possible pair of neurons, the algorithm either define a connection or not. Therefore, the performance evaluation can be assessed with the usual metrics of machine learning like Receiver Operating Characteristic (ROC) and Precision Recall (PR) curves. The ChaLearn Connectomics proposes as a global metric the use of the area under the ROC curve (AUC), however, ROC curves can present an overly optimistic view of an algorithm's performance if there is a large skew in the class distribution, as typically encountered in sparse network problems. To tackle this problem, precision-recall (PR) curves have been proposed as an alternative to ROC curves Sabes and Jordan (1995). For this reason, we present in Table 1 the Area Under PR curve (AUPR) and compare our method with GTE and the state-of-the-art combination of these features *Ranksum*. The results of GTE are obtained with the software available online

Table 1 Area Under Precision Recall scores for each inference method at the datasets of the connectomics challenge (the higher the better). The Ranksum makes use of the original pairwise inferred networks while our method use the symmetrized GTE (denoted as I^*). The best statistically significant results tested with a Wilcoxon test are highlighted

	I GTE	II corr	III $CT_{0.1\%}$	IV $RD_{0.1\%}$	V $MD_{0.1\%}$	CS (I^*, III, VI, V)	$RS\,(I, III, VI, V)$
highcc	0.163	0.051	0.088	0.166	0.125	*0.330*	0.184
highcon	0.199	0.030	0.120	0.125	0.073	*0.241*	0.184
iNet1-Size100-CC01inh	*0.242*	0.117	0.117	0.106	0.123	0.180	0.158
iNet1-Size100-CC02inh	*0.247*	0.113	0.150	0.103	0.120	0.223	0.181
iNet1-Size100-CC03inh	*0.333*	0.116	0.198	0.130	0.131	0.314	0.237
iNet1-Size100-CC04inh	*0.398*	0.120	0.206	0.187	0.158	0.394	0.297
iNet1-Size100-CC05inh	0.366	0.120	0.208	0.288	0.179	*0.423*	0.366
iNet1-Size100-CC06inh	0.538	0.204	0.188	0.371	0.318	*0.582*	0.480
lowcc	0.085	0.015	0.085	0.031	0.022	*0.126*	0.083
lowcon	0.093	0.023	0.025	0.024	0.031	*0.196*	0.125
normal-1	0.164	0.028	0.085	0.110	0.061	*0.251*	0.155
normal-2	0.169	0.028	0.105	0.095	0.048	*0.242*	0.153
normal-3-highrate	0.201	0.057	0.037	0.143	0.073	*0.293*	0.181
normal-3	0.193	0.025	0.098	0.094	0.044	*0.260*	0.150
normal-4-lownoise	0.141	0.030	0.120	0.086	0.053	*0.271*	0.156
normal-4	0.139	0.026	0.085	0.082	0.046	*0.254*	0.140
Mean	0.229	0.069	0.120	0.134	0.100	*0.286*	0.202

dherkova (2014) using as conditioning levels the values $\{0.05, 0.10\}$ for the iNet1-Size100-CC's networks and $\{0.15, 0.20\}$ for the big datasets. We have also computed a statistical test to discard non-significant results. First, we compute the contribution of each link to the area under the curve and then we apply the Wilcoxon test on the resulting vectors Hollander et al. (2013). If the best result of each dataset have a p-value smaller than 5% it is typed in italic font and boldfaced.

Table 1 shows the performance of our individual networks ($CT_{0.1\%}, MD_{0.1\%}, RD$) and we can observe that it depends on the properties of the network (high/low-connectivity or high/low-activity).

We also compare our community based approach with the state-of-the-art Ranksum approach, which is shown at the last column. Note that the Ranksum makes use of the original pairwise derived networks and our method used the symmetrized GTE (denoted as I^*). We can observe that our normalization and simple combination is able to improve the quality of the individual recovered networks and also improves the state-of-the-art community Ranksum. As shown in the table, our approach is competitive even though our method does not recover a directed network as GTE does. It is worth noting that using AUC as a metric we obtain similar conclusions. The table with AUC results is available in the Supplementary Material Bellot and Meyer (2014).

Additionally to the results shown at Table 1 we also have used our method in the test and validation networks where the network is unknown. Using the connectomics submission tool we obtain 0.90402 score of Area under the ROC curve, and we would have been ranked in the 30th position.

As stated previously the big advantage of our method is the low complexity $O(n^2)$. The CPU time needed to compute the different features for the big datasets in a 2 x Intel Xeon E5 2670 8C (2.6 GHz), has a mean of 1282.86 min for the GTE, 3.31 min for $CT_{0.1\%}$, 66.53 min for $MD_{0.1\%}$ and 21.17 min for RD. The process of CLRsum is almost instantaneous once we have the individual features, and therefore the computation time is the sum of the time needed to compute the individual features. Hence, our proposal improves GTE with a negligible overload of time.

5 Conclusion

An unsupervised network inference method for neural connectomics has been presented. This method improves the state-of-the-art network inference method GTE relying on CLRsum consensus among GTE and three new informative features.

We have compared our method experimentally to two state-of-the-art network inference methods, namely GTE and correlation network, on the connectomics challenge datasets. The experimental results showed that our proposal is competitive with state-of-the-art algorithms.

Acknowledgements This work has been partially supported by the Spanish "MECD" FPU Research Fellowship, the Spanish "MICINN" project TEC2013-43935-R and the Cellex foundation.

References

Pau Bellot and Patrick E Meyer. Efficient combination of pairwise feature networks - supplemental material. http://bellot.geek-lab.org/publications/efficient-combination-of-pairwise-feature-networks, 2014. Accessed: 2014-07-22.

Atul J Butte and Isaac S Kohane. Mutual information relevance networks: functional genomic clustering using pairwise entropy measurements. In *Pac Symp Biocomput*, volume 5, pages 418–429, 2000.

dherkova. Transfer entropy - causality. https://github.com/dherkova/TE-Causality/tree/connectomics_challenge, 2014. Accessed: 2014-06-01.

Jeremiah J Faith, Boris Hayete, Joshua T Thaden, Ilaria Mogno, Jamey Wierzbowski, Guillaume Cottarel, Simon Kasif, James J Collins, and Timothy S Gardner. Large-scale mapping and validation of escherichia coli transcriptional regulation from a compendium of expression profiles. *PLoS biology*, 5(1):e8, 2007.

Myles Hollander, Douglas A Wolfe, and Eric Chicken. *Nonparametric statistical methods*, volume 751. John Wiley & Sons, 2013.

Dominik Janzing, Patrik O. Hoyer, and Bernhard Schlkopf. Telling cause from effect based on high-dimensional observations, 2010.

Daniel Marbach, James C Costello, Robert Küffner, Nicole M Vega, Robert J Prill, Diogo M Camacho, Kyle R Allison, Manolis Kellis, James J Collins, Gustavo Stolovitzky, et al. Wisdom of crowds for robust gene network inference. *Nature methods*, 9(8):796–804, 2012.

Adam A Margolin, Ilya Nemenman, Katia Basso, Chris Wiggins, Gustavo Stolovitzky, Riccardo D Favera, and Andrea Califano. Aracne: an algorithm for the reconstruction of gene regulatory networks in a mammalian cellular context. *BMC bioinformatics*, 7(Suppl 1):S7, 2006.

Patrick E Meyer, Kevin Kontos, Frederic Lafitte, and Gianluca Bontempi. Information-theoretic inference of large transcriptional regulatory networks. *EURASIP journal on bioinformatics and systems biology*, page 79879, 2007.

The modENCODE Consortium et al. Identification of functional elements and regulatory circuits by drosophila modencode. *Science*, 330(6012):1787–1797, 2010.

Alessio Moneta and Peter Spirtes. Graph-based search procedure for vector autoregressive models. Technical report, LEM Working Paper Series, 2005.

Guido Nolte and Klaus-Robert Müller. Localizing and estimating causal relations of interacting brain rhythms. *Frontiers in human neuroscience*, 4, 2010.

Judea Pearl. *Causality: models, reasoning and inference*, volume 29. Cambridge Univ Press, 2000.

Florin Popescu and Isabelle Guyon, editors. *Causality in Time Series: Challenges in Machine Learning*, volume 5. Microtome, 2013.

Philip N Sabes and Michael I Jordan. Advances in neural information processing systems. In *In G. Tesauro & D. Touretzky & T. Leed (Eds.), Advances in Neural Information Processing Systems*. Citeseer, 1995.

Thomas Schreiber. Measuring information transfer. *Physical review letters*, 85(2):461, 2000.

Olav Stetter, Demian Battaglia, Jordi Soriano, and Theo Geisel. Model-free reconstruction of excitatory neuronal connectivity from calcium imaging signals. *PLoS Comput Biol*, 8(8):e1002653, 08 2012.

Predicting Spiking Activities in DLS Neurons with Linear-Nonlinear-Poisson Model

Sisi Ma and David J. Barker

Editors: Demian Battaglia, Isabelle Guyon, Vincent Lemaire, Javier Orlandi, Bisakha Ray, Jordi Soriano

Abstract Spike train generation in primary motor cortex (M1) and somatosensory cortex (S1) has been studied extensively and is relatively well understood. On the contrary, the functionality and physiology of the dorsolateral striatum (DLS), the immediate downstream region of M1 and S1 and a critical link in the motor circuit, still requires intensive investigation. In the current study, spike trains of individual DLS neurons were reconstructed using a Linear-Nonlinear-Poisson model with features from two modalities: (1) the head position modality, which contains information regarding head movement and proprioception of the animal's head; (2) the spike history modality, which contains information regarding the intrinsic physiological properties of the neuron. For the majority of the neurons examined, viable reconstruction accuracy was achieved when the neural activity was modeled with either feature modality or the two feature modalities combined. Subpopulations of neurons were also identified that had better reconstruction accuracy when modeled with features from single modalities. This study demonstrates the feasibility of spike train reconstruction in DLS neurons and provides insights into the physiology of DLS neurons.

The original form of this article appears in JMLR W&CP Volume 46.

S. Ma (✉)
Center of Health Informatics and Bioinformatics, NYU Medical Center,
227 E 30th Street, New York, NY 10016, USA
e-mail: Sisi.Ma@nyumc.org

D.J. Barker
National Institute on Drug Abuse, Neuronal Networks Section,
National Institute of Health, Baltimore, MD 20892, USA
e-mail: David.Barker@nih.gov

© Springer International Publishing AG 2017   95
D. Battaglia et al. (eds.), *Neural Connectomics Challenge*, The Springer Series
on Challenges in Machine Learning, DOI 10.1007/978-3-319-53070-3_8

Keywords Spike train reconstruction · Dorsolateral striatum · Motor circuit

1   Introduction

1.1   Dorsolateral Striatum Single Body Part Neurons

Motor commands initiated by motor neurons in M1 descend to the spinal cord and result in the flexion or extension of their corresponding muscle groups. These motor neurons also send an efferent copy of motor commands to the DLS (corresponds to the dorsolateral caudate-putamen in human), the input structure for the basal ganglia. Similarly, the DLS receives inputs from S1. Information from the DLS is further relayed through globus pallidus, thalamus, premotor cortex and back to M1. This motor loop is thought to be involved in monitoring and providing feedback for ongoing movements (Alexander et al. 1986; Cohen et al. 2010). Moreover, a number of diseases involving motor or sensorimotor impairment, including Parkinson's and Huntington's disease, feature disrupted DLS function (Georgiou-Karistianis and Egan 2011; Kordower et al. 2013). Thus, understanding DLS functionality may lead to new diagnostic and therapeutic methods for these diseases.

   Previous studies discovered single body part correlated neurons (SBP neurons) in the DLS. These neurons are tuned to single body parts and specific movement features (e.g. distance, duration, velocity, and starting position) for that body part (Crutcher and DeLong 1984; Crutcher and Alexander 1990; Cho and West 1997; Tang et al. 2007; Ma et al. 2013). Current methods for identifying movement correlates used in these studies involves defining movement features and categorizing movements according to those features. However, if movement features are incorrectly defined (i.e. not defined according to features the neurons are sensitive to), or if movements were categorized into categories that are too broad, a significant amount of information might be lost. To avoid this problem, the current study used the raw position data without arbitrarily defining movement features and applies a Linear-Nonlinear-Poisson Model to predict the neural activities in the DLS.

1.2   The Linear-Nonlinear-Poisson Model

The Linear-Nonlinear-Poisson Model (the LNP model) is commonly used to model the process of spiking activity. Ample studies have reported successes in predicting single neurons' activities in sensory neurons by the LNP model (up to 82% accuracy) (Schwartz et al. 2006; Pillow et al. 2008). The LNP model can simultaneously capture variables from different modalities that may influence the spiking activity of a neuron with high efficiency. Variables from two modalities are often considered when predicting spiking activities: (1) the extrinsic stimulus that the neuron may respond to or encode, (2) the spike history of the neuron. The LNP model first applies a linear filter (the linear part of the LNP) to the extrinsic stimulus and/or spike history. Then, the filtered responses are summed and exponentiated (the non-linear part of the LNP) to obtain an instantaneous spike rate. The instantaneous spike rate is the parameter of the Poisson distribution that determines spiking activity (Poisson part of the LNP). The parameters of the model were fitted with maximum likelihood estimation. In the present study, head position record (extrinsic stimulus) and spike history data were used to predict spiking activities of individual neurons in the DLS, using the LNP model as classifier. The result of the study indicated that it is possible to predict spiking activity using the LNP model in the DLS, despite the fact that the DLS does not interact with extrinsic stimulus (the head positions) directly, but instead only receives information from primary motor and sensory areas. Also, results show that the head position record and spike history data contribute differently when predicting the spiking activities for individual neurons.

2   Methods

2.1   Data Collection and Preprocessing

The current study reanalyzed data previously published in Pawlak et al. (2010), where details regarding data collection can be found. Briefly, the dataset consists of extracellular single neural recordings of 47 neurons from 13 rats. All neurons were histologically confirmed to be located in the DLS. Recordings from these neurons lasted one hour, during which time the animals were walking on a treadmill and producing head movements primarily in the vertical direction. The position (x, y coordinates) of the animal's head was measured by a video camera (60 Hz) facing the treadmill. The action potentials (spike train) were simultaneously recorded with 50 kHz sampling frequency.

The primary goal of the present study was to determine the feasibility of reconstructing the spike train, i.e. to predict whether or not a spike occurs in a short time interval, using head position and spike history data as predictors. An interval of 16.7 ms was used, since the position records of the head was obtained at a 60 Hz sampling rate. More specifically, the neural activity was binned into 16.7 ms intervals and then converted to binary and used as the outcome for prediction, such that equal number of observations for position record and neural activity were obtained for a given neuron.

2.2 Experimental Design

2.2.1 Predicting Neural Activity with Features from All Modalities

Firstly, features from both head position history (*hp*) and spike history (*spkh*) were used to predict neural activity at time t. For this analysis, position record m time bins before time t was used, i.e. $hp_{t-m}, hp_{t-m+1}, \ldots, hp_{t-1}$. Similarly, spike history data was used up to m time bins before, i.e. $spkh_{t-m}, spkh_{t-m+1}, \ldots, spkh_{t-1}$. The LNP model is expressed as the following:

$$\lambda(t) = \exp(hp\_filter \cdot hp(t) + spkh\_filter \cdot spkh(t)).$$

$\lambda(t)$ is the rate of the Poisson distribution that generates the spike at time t. $hp\_filter \cdot hp(t)$ is a linear projection of $hp(t)$, the head position record m time bins before time t, onto the receptive field of the neuron, as defined by the linear filter for the head position hp_filter. Similarly, $spkh\_filter \cdot spkh(t)$ is $spkh(t)$, the spike history m time bins before time t, convolved with the spike history filter.

Cross validation was utilized to select parameter m for individual neuron's individual data split. Data from individual neurons were split into splits of 10 min, resulting in 6 data splits that were consecutive in time. The model was first trained on data split s, performance was validated on split $s + 1$, with $s \in [1, 2, 3, 4]$. Parameter m that resulted in the best performance, as measured by AUC, on the validation set was selected. AUC is the area under precision recall curve constructed by comparing the true occurrence of the spike versus the instantaneous firing rate $\lambda(t)$. The LNP model was then retrained on data from split s and $s + 1$. The resulting model was tested data split $s + 2$. The average AUCs over the four testing sets was obtained for every neuron. In addition, permutation tests was conducted to determine whether the prediction performance on the testing sets were significantly better than random for every neuron.

2.2.2 Comparing Performances of Different Feature Modalities

The relative importance of different data modalities, i.e. head position and spike history, was then evaluated by constructing classification models with data from either modality separately. The training, validation and testing of the models was similar as described in Sect. 2.2.1. Permutation tests were conducted to determine whether the differences in AUCs between model using head position modality versus model using spike history modality was significantly better than random.

2.2.3 Comparing Performances of Single Modality Versus All Modalities

Lastly, the possible improvement of performance by combining features from multiple modalities was examined. AUC resulting from models using features from all modalities were compared with the best AUC resulting from models using features from any single modality. Permutation tests was conducted to determine whether the differences in AUCs was significantly better than random. The p values resulting from all permutation tests were FDR adjusted globally to correct for multiple comparisons.

3 Results

3.1 Predicting Neural Activity with Features from All Modalities

When using features from all available modalities, i.e. head position and spike history, significantly better than random AUCs were achieved in 44 out of 47 neurons. The distributions of average AUCs for individual neurons were shown in Fig. 1a. Notice that about 40% of the neurons have AUCs between 0.5 and 0.6, the majority of which were significantly better than random, indicating small yet significant signal.

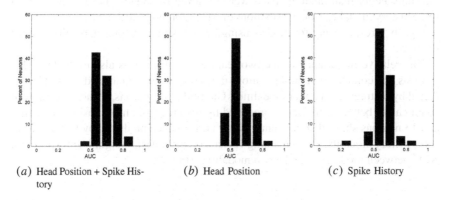

(*a*) Head Position + Spike History   (*b*) Head Position   (*c*) Spike History

Fig. 1 Distribution of AUCs predicted by different feature modalities

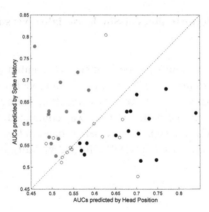

Fig. 2 AUCs predicted by head position features versus those predicted by spike history features: Each *dot* represents one neuron. *Open circles* represent neurons with similar AUCs when predicted by head position features or spike history features. *Grey dots* represent neurons that have significantly higher AUCs predicted by spike history. *Black dots* represent neurons that have significantly higher AUCs predicted by head position

3.2 Predicting Neural Activity with Features from Individual Modalities

In 32 out of 47 neurons, significantly better than random AUCs were achieved by models using features from head position modality. In 35 out of 47 neurons, significantly better than random AUCs were achieved by models using features from spike history modality. The distributions of AUCs for individual neurons were shown in Fig. 1b, c respectively for models using head position features and spike history features.

The relative importance of the two feature modalities was also evaluated. This analysis was conducted in the 41 neurons that showed better than random AUCs predicted by features from either modalities. Out of the 41 neurons, 15 neurons showed significantly better performance predicted by features from head position modality and 13 neurons showed significantly better performance predicted by features from spike history modality. The remaining 13 neurons did not show significantly different AUC between models using the two modalities (Fig. 2).

3.3 Comparing Performances of Single Modality Versus All Modalities Combined

There are a total number of 45 neurons that showed significantly better than random AUCs obtained from models using either single modalities or all modalities. Out of

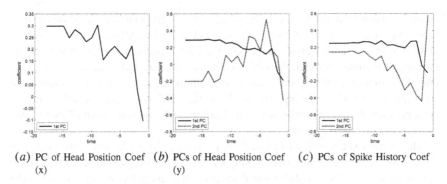

(a) PC of Head Position Coef (x)   (b) PCs of Head Position Coef (y)   (c) PCs of Spike History Coef

Fig. 3 The top principal components of the linear coefficients

these 45 neurons, 9 of the neurons show a significant improvement in AUC when modeled with features from all modalities.

4 Discussion

The current study illustrated the feasibility of reconstructing the neural activity in majority of DLS neurons. One of the advantages of using the LNP model as classifier is that it implicitly keeps the temporal structure of the features, which is well-suited for time series data. Another advantage of the LNP model is that the linear coefficients of the model depict the typical sequences of head position or spike history leading to spikes. Principal component analysis was conducted on the linear coefficients of the LNP models for individual neurons to identify common patterns. Principal components (PCs) that explain more than 10% variability were plotted (Fig. 3). The first PC for both horizontal (x coordinates) and vertical (y coordinates) head position indicates that one of the position sequence that triggers a spike is a abrupt movement in one direction (Fig. 3a, b). For the vertical head position, the second PC indicates that a relatively slow movement with a change in direction may trigger spikes (Fig. 3b). For the spike history, the first PC indicates a relatively rapid change in spiking activity often precedes a spike, while the second PC indicates that a slow change in spiking activity followed by a rapid reversal in spiking activity often precedes a spike (Fig. 3c).

The current study identified subpopulations of neurons that primarily correlate with different feature modalities. The proportion of neurons that are identified to be correlated with head position history is higher (32 out of 47) when compared to traditional methods (less than 25%) which require categorizing movements according to some movement features (e.g. direction, distance, velocity, duration). Specifically, traditional methods examine neural activity for categorized movements and compare this activity to activity during both other movement categories or non-movement (baseline control). In this method, neurons are identified as movement related if their firing rates in one or more of the pre-defined categories are different when compared to the non-movement baseline. In contrast, the LNP model does not arbitrarily define movement features. Instead, the LNP model uses the raw data and maximum likelihood estimation to determine what head position sequences (i.e. movements) are most likely to result in spiking activity. Thus, the LNP model may be able to utilize head position data at its full resolution, leading to the identification of more head movement correlated neurons.

The current study failed to identify improvement in prediction performance in most of the neurons examined when using features from both modalities. It is possible that in some cases the two data modalities contain overlapping information (e.g. the spike history may encode the head movement history). Alternatively, it is possible that one of the modalities does not contain any information regarding the outcome (e.g. the neuron might not be related to the movement of the head, therefore incorporating the head movement history data does not help the prediction).

In conclusion, the current study demonstrated the feasibility of predicting the neural activity in DLS using the LNP model. Also, for individual neurons, the present data show that specific feature modalities contribute differently when predicting neural activity. The relative importance of feature modalities provide insights into the response characteristics of individual neurons.

Acknowledgements The Authors thank Dr. Alexander Statnikov and Dr. Sara Solla for their constructive input in experimental design and Dr. Anthony Pawlak for providing the data. This work was partially supported by NRSA grant DA 032270 and Rutgers special study award.

References

Garrett E Alexander, Mahlon R DeLong, and Peter L Strick. Parallel organization of functionally segregated circuits linking basal ganglia and cortex. *Annual review of neuroscience*, 9(1):357–381, 1986.

Jeiwon Cho and Mark O West. Distributions of single neurons related to body parts in the lateral striatum of the rat. *Brain research*, 756(1):241–246, 1997.

Oren Cohen, Efrat Sherman, Nofya Zinger, Steve Perlmutter, and Yifat Prut. Getting ready to move: transmitted information in the corticospinal pathway during preparation for movement. *Current opinion in neurobiology*, 20(6):696–703, 2010.

MD Crutcher and MR DeLong. Single cell studies of the primate putamen. *Experimental Brain Research*, 53(2):244–258, 1984.

Michael D Crutcher and Garrett E Alexander. Movement-related neuronal activity selectively coding either direction or muscle pattern in three motor areas of the monkey. *J Neurophysiol*, 64(1):151–163, 1990.

Nellie Georgiou-Karistianis and Gary F Egan. Connectivity-based segmentation of the striatum in huntington's disease: vulnerability of motor pathways. *Neurobiology of disease*, 42(3):475–481, 2011.

Jeffrey H Kordower, C Warren Olanow, Hemraj B Dodiya, Yaping Chu, Thomas G Beach, Charles H Adler, Glenda M Halliday, and Raymond T Bartus. Disease duration and the integrity of the nigrostriatal system in parkinson's disease. *Brain*, 136(8):2419–2431, 2013.

Sisi Ma, Anthony P Pawlak, Jeiwon Cho, David H Root, David J Barker, and Mark O West. Amphetamine's dose-dependent effects on dorsolateral striatum sensorimotor neuron firing. *Behavioural brain research*, 244:152–161, 2013.

Anthony P Pawlak, Chris C Tang, Cathy Pederson, Martin B Wolske, and Mark O West. Acute effects of cocaine on movement-related firing of dorsolateral striatal neurons depend on predrug firing rate and dose. *Journal of Pharmacology and Experimental Therapeutics*, 332(2):667–683, 2010.

Jonathan W Pillow, Jonathon Shlens, Liam Paninski, Alexander Sher, Alan M Litke, EJ Chichilnisky, and Eero P Simoncelli. Spatio-temporal correlations and visual signalling in a complete neuronal population. *Nature*, 454(7207):995–999, 2008.

Odelia Schwartz, Jonathan W Pillow, Nicole C Rust, and Eero P Simoncelli. Spike-triggered neural characterization. *Journal of Vision*, 6(4):13, 2006.

Chengke Tang, Anthony P Pawlak, Volodymyr Prokopenko, and Mark O West. Changes in activity of the striatum during formation of a motor habit. *European Journal of Neuroscience*, 25(4):1212–1227, 2007.

SuperSlicing Frame Restoration
for Anisotropic ssTEM and Video Data

Dmitry Laptev and Joachim M. Buhmann

*Editors: Demian Battaglia, Isabelle Guyon, Vincent Lemaire,
Javier Orlandi, Bisakha Ray, Jordi Soriano*

Abstract In biological imaging the data is often represented by a sequence of anisotropic frames — the resolution in one dimension is significantly lower than in the other dimensions. E.g. in electron microscopy it arises from the thickness of a scanned section. This leads to blurred images and raises problems in tasks like neuronal image segmentation. We present the details and additional evaluation of an approach originally introduced in Laptev et al. IEEE 11th International Symposium on Biomedical Imaging ISBI 2014. IEEE Xplore (2014) called SUPERSLICING to decompose the observed frame into a sequence of plausible *hidden sub-frames*. Based on sub-frame decomposition by SUPERSLICING we propose a novel automated method to perform neuronal structure segmentation. We test our approach on a popular connectomics benchmark, where SUPERSLICING preserves topological structures significantly better than other algorithms. We also generalize the approach for video anisotropicity that comes from the long exposure time and show that our method outperforms baseline methods on a reconstruction of low frame rate videos of natural scenes.

Keywords Anisotropic data · Super resolution · Connectomics · Segmentation · Registration

The original form of this article appears in JMLR W&CP Volume 46.

D. Laptev (✉) · J.M. Buhmann
Department of Computer Science, ETH Zurich, 8092 Zurich, Switzerland
e-mail: dlaptev@inf.ethz.ch

J.M. Buhmann
e-mail: jbuhmann@inf.ethz.ch

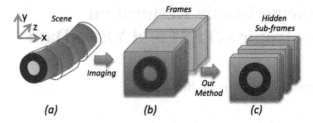

Fig. 1 A schematic illustration of our approach: **a** neuronal structure in brain tissue sample; **b** the tissue sample is cut and captured with ssTEM, producing anisotropic frames with blur; **c** the proposed method SUPERSLICING reconstructs *hidden sub-frames* with sharp details

1 Introduction

Digital imaging defines a quantization of the visual appearance of the world. The intensity of a pixel is the *cumulative* energy that has reached the physical sensor. In consequence, the details of a scene that are smaller than the spatial resolution of the sensor are getting *averaged away* (Fig. 1). Visually, averaging overcomes the problem of aliasing, but causes spatial blur and such data is called *anisotropic*.

Serial section transmission electron microscopy (ssTEM) Cardona et al. (2010) of brain tissue is an important example. This method is the only available technique that guarantees sufficient resolution for reconstructing neuronal structures on the synapse level and, thereby, supports the scientific goals of connectomics Seung (2012) to understand brain functions. This technique renders the volume in a highly *anisotropic* way — the resolution across vertical dimension of the stack (thickness) is much lower than that of the horizontal dimensions.

The same phenomenon can be found in a low frame rate video recording. In case of *anisotropic video*[1] one can interpret the captured frame as an average of *hidden subframes* captured with shorter exposure time. The goal is then is to increase temporal resolution: estimate a high frame rate video from low frame rate.

We propose a method called SUPERSLICING (Super resolution frame Slicing). It reconstructs isotropic *hidden subframes* from a sequence of anisotropic frames, thereby increasing the depth or temporal resolution. This reconstruction states an inherently ill-posed problem as there exists an infinite number of possible sub-frames that can produce the same observed frame. We propose a regularisation that uses the information from the neighboring frames to resolve these ambiguities. The problem is formulated as energy minimization which appears to be convex and therefore guarantees the global optimum. The objective function is guided by two principal considerations: (i) the physical constraints of the imaging process; (ii) the structures in sub-frames should follow the correspondence between structures in the neighboring frames. To formalize the latter SUPERSLICING uses optical flow to find the correspondences between neighboring frames and interpolates them into sub-frames.

---

[1]Video is called *anisotropic* or *full-exposure* if exposure time equals to the time between two frames.

SUPERSLICING enables us to propose a novel automated method to perform neuronal structure segmentation (Sect. 4). It recovers the crisp image of these structures and facilitates recognition of neural structures. The experiments on Drosophila first instar larva ventral nerve cord (VNC) dataset Cardona et al. (2010) demonstrate significant improvement over the baselines.

2   Related Work

The first group of related techniques for frame enhancement interpolates between two neighboring frames. The simplest approach is a linear frame interpolation, which, although simple and fast, produces blurry results even when the initial frames are sharp. A more advanced technique Baker et al. (2011) is based on optical flow estimation and frame warping. However, in anisotropic data, frames are often reconstructed as blurred as initial frames because it takes into account no constraints on how imaging is performed. In contrast, SUPERSLICING reconstructs the changes *within* the frame, therefore recovering crisp details in each sub-frame. We use both of these approaches as baselines in our experiments.

Another approach Hu et al. (2012) to solving the problem of spatial enhancement relies on using multiple ssTEM projections. Unlike these methods, we are considering a more general case and use only one sequence of frames from one ssTEM stack. And the third type of approaches Shimano et al. (2010) is based on exploring the recurrence of small self-similar patches in space and time. However, these methods assume that similar patches appear repeatedly within the frame sequence which is almost never the case for neuronal structures. In contrast to these methods we do not rely on high recurrence of self-similar patches and therefore, we solve a more general problem.

Neuronal structure segmentation and recognition has two general approaches. The first approach Kaynig et al. (2010) focuses on the detection of neuron membranes in each section independently based only on local information around every pixel. The second approach Laptev et al. (2012) incorporates context from different sections to resolve ambiguities that cannot be resolved within one section. The biggest challenge for the segmentation algorithm is posed by the blurry membranes (see Fig. 5), that are often the result of anisotropy. We propose a novel method that first recovers the sharp sub-frames of a slice using SUPERSLICING and then uses them to perform segmentation. As the recovered sub-frames contain finer details the segmentation algorithm is able to identify the neuronal structures with higher accuracy than methods without SUPERSLICING (Fig. 2).

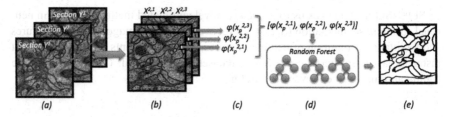

Fig. 2 An illustration of the SUPERSLICING pipeline for neuronal structures segmentation. Based on the non-linear correspondings between neighboring frames Y^1, Y^2 and Y^3 (**a**) the algorithm evaluates hidden sub-frames $X^{2,1}$, $X^{2,2}$, $X^{2,3}$ (**b**). Then, feature vectors in sub-frame pixels are evaluated: $\varphi(x_p^{n,1}), \ldots, \varphi(x_p^{n,L})$ (**c**). After that the method concatenates them and passes the concatenated feature vector to a RF classifier (**d**) that returns the final segmentation (**e**)

3 Proposed Method

Let Y^n be the observed sequence of frames, $n \in [1, \ldots, N]$, y_p^n – pixel p of the frame Y^n, $i(y_p^n)$ – the intensity of pixel y_p^n. Let $\epsilon(x_p^n)$ be a set of neighbors of pixel x_p^n. We want to reconstruct L *hidden sub-frames* $X^{n,l}$, $l \in [1, \ldots, L]$ of the observed frames Y^n.

3.1 Optimization Task

We define optimization problem Eq. 1 to approximate *hidden sub-frames* as an energy minimization problem for given correspondences Ω. The energy Eq. 1 consists of three terms. The first term, the data term, represents the physical constraints that the observed frame should be equal to the average of the *hidden sub-frames*: $i(y_p^n) = \frac{1}{L} \sum_{l=1}^{L} i(x_p^{n,l})$, $\forall y_p^n \in Y^n$.

The second term promotes smoothness by favoring an alignment of pixel's intensities in the sub-frames along the structure's progression between the frames. The algorithm proceeds by finding correspondences between the anisotropic frames using optical flow and then interpolates them into the sub-frames using bilinear interpolation (see Sect. 3.2).

The third term encourages the resulting sub-frames to be smooth to avoid visual artefacts. This goal is achieved by minimizing the difference of intensities between the neighboring pixels.

$$E(X^{n,1}, \ldots, X^{n,L}) = \sum_{y \in Y^n} \left(i(y) - \frac{1}{L} \sum_{l=1}^{L} i(x_p^{n,l}) \right)^2 + \lambda \sum_{(\hat{x}_p^{n,l}, \hat{x}_q^{n,l+1}) \in \Omega} \left(\sum_{x \in \epsilon(\hat{x}_p^{n,l})} w(x, \hat{x}_p^{n,l}) i(x) \right.$$
$$\left. - \sum_{x \in \epsilon(\hat{x}_q^{n,l+1})} w(x, \hat{x}_q^{n,l+1}) i(x) \right)^2 + \gamma \sum_{\substack{x_p^{n,l}; x_q^{n,l} \in \epsilon(x_p^{n,l}) \\ l=1, \ldots, L}} \left(i(x_p^{n,l}) - i(x_q^{n,l}) \right)^2. \quad (1)$$

Here λ and γ are Lagrange parameters that control the degree of regularization versus data fidelity. This is a quadratic functional with respect to $i(x_q^{n,l})$ and therefore we can achieve *global optimum* with any convex optimization technique (we used interior point method in our experiments).

3.2 Corresponding Pixels

How can we find the set Ω of corresponding pixels? A central idea of this paper is to utilize the context of neighboring frames for reconstructing sub-frames. We first find the correspondences between the pixels in neighboring frames and only after these constraints have been identified, we interpolate these correspondences through sub-frames.

Assume that we observe the sequence of three images: $Y^1, Y^2 \equiv Y, Y^3$. For every pixel y_p^2 of y^2 we find the corresponding pixel y_p^k from image $y^k, k \in \{1, 3\}$ by finding the set $\Omega_Y^k = \{(y_p^2, y_q^k)|\forall y_p^2 \in Y^2\}$ minimizing optical flow energy:

$$E_{fl}(\Omega_Y^k) = \sum_{y_p \in Y} \left(i(y_p) - i(y_q^k) \right)^2 + \alpha \sum_{y_p \in Y^2} \rho(y_p, y_q^k)^2.$$

Here α is a model parameter, $\rho(y_p, y_q)$ is euclidean distance between the pixels y_p and y_q in pixel grid. Optical flow results in good correspondences, even though it allows only integer displacements, because the membrane displacements are smooth and need to be estimated only up to the thickness of a membrane, which is on average 3 to 7 pixels.

As soon as we have corresponding sets Ω_Y^1 and Ω_Y^3, we can draw a curve φ through y_p^1 to y_q^2 and y_t^3 for every two correspondings (y_p^1, y_q^2) and (y_q^2, y_t^3). Then we interpolate the pixels curve φ crosses in hidden sub-slices: $\hat{x}_{\varphi(1)}^1, \ldots, \hat{x}_{\varphi(L)}^L$ (see Fig. 3). Then $\Omega_\varphi = \{(\hat{x}_{\varphi(l)}^l, \hat{x}_{\varphi(l+1)}^{l+1})|l \in [1, \ldots, L-1]\}$. The final set Ω is a union of all sets Ω_φ.

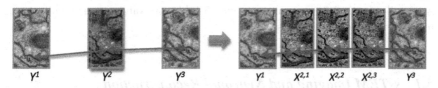

$Y^1 \qquad Y^2 \qquad Y^3 \qquad\qquad Y^1 \quad X^{2,1} \quad X^{2,2} \quad X^{2,3} \quad Y^3$

Fig. 3 An illustration of correspondence interpolation. *Left arrows* show correspondences between original frames; *right arrows* shows interpolated correspondences between sub-frames. The second term of the energy function encourages the corresponding pixels to have low difference in intensities

If pixel $\hat{x}_p^{n,l}$ does not fit to the pixel grid, we employ the bilinear interpolation technique and rewrite it as a weighted sum of direct neighbors in a grid $\hat{x}_p^{n,l} = \sum_{x \in \epsilon(\hat{x}_p^{n,l})} w(x, \hat{x}_p^{n,l}) x$, $w(.) \geq 0$, $\sum_{x \in \epsilon(\hat{x}_p^{n,l})} w(x, \hat{x}_p^{n,l}) = 1$. Here $w(x_1, x_2)$ is a bilinear weight that is closer to 1 if the distance between x_1 and x_2 is small and closer to 0 otherwise. We then write the second set of constraints enforcing that corresponding pixels of sub-frames assume the same intensity:

$$\sum_{x \in \epsilon(\hat{x}_p^{n,l})} w(x, \hat{x}_p^{n,l}) i(x) = \sum_{x \in \epsilon(\hat{x}_q^{n,l+1})} w(x, \hat{x}_q^{n,l+1}) i(x),$$

$\forall (\hat{x}_p^{n,l}, \hat{x}_q^{n,l+1}) \in \Omega$, where Ω is a set of all pairs of corresponding pixels.

4   Neuronal Segmentation

We propose a method that first reconstructs hidden sub-frames and uses features that are evaluated in pixels of recovered sub-frames for classification. Our workflow is illustrated in Fig. 2. For a given section Y^n we first recover sub-frames $X^{n,1}, \ldots, X^{n,L}$ with SUPERSLICING. Then, for every pixel $x_p^{n,l}$, $l \in [1, \ldots, L]$ we calculate features $\varphi(x_p^{n,l})$, concatenate the feature vectors and use this extended feature vector as input to a Random Forest (RF) classifier Breiman (2001).

We select the method parameters γ and λ as well as optical flow parameter α with cross validation. We use RF with 255 trees and perform training on 10% of all the pixels. As features we use per pixel SIFT histograms Lowe (1999) and line filter transforms Sandberg and Brega (2007) with different parameters.

5   Experiments

To evaluate our approach we perform experiments on several different tasks and datasets. For all of the following experiments we select the method parameters γ and λ as well as optical flow parameter α with 5-fold cross validation and with respect to the corresponding metric used.

5.1   ssTEM Imaging and Neuronal Reconstruction

We use publicly available segmentation challenge dataset Cardona et al. (2010). Figures 4 and 5 qualitatively shows the results of our algorithm for hidden frame recovery. Membranes recovered in the sub-frames using SUPERSLICING are much sharper than the ones produced by the baseline methods.

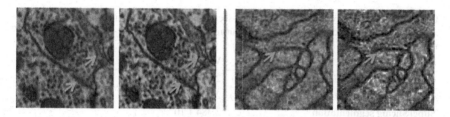

Fig. 4 Two fragments of neuronal tissue captured with ssTEM: original sections (*left*) and one of sub-frames (*right*). *Arrows* point out membranes that were blurred out in the original images and appear more visible after sub-frame decomposition

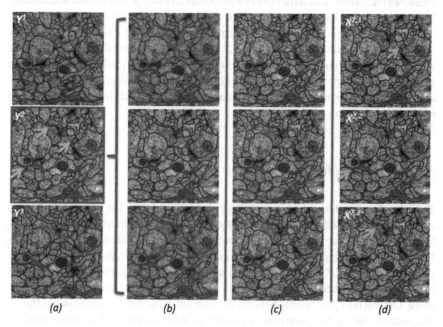

Fig. 5 A qualitative comparison of our method with the baselines. Column **a** shows original anisotropic sections. Three following column shows $L = 3$ interpolated frames estimated with: linear interpolation (**b**), optical flow warping (**c**), SUPERSLICING (**d**). *Arrows* point out blurred membranes that are better visible after sub-frame reconstruction

To quantitatively test the approach for neuronal membrane segmentation presented in Sect. 4, we compare segmentation results with two more methods: RF segmentation based on only features evaluated in one layer Kaynig et al. (2010), and RF segmentation based on context from neighboring sections Laptev et al. (2012). For fair comparison we implement the same set of features for all three methods and use the same RF structure with no post-processing to measure the impact of SUPERSLICING.

As we care about neurons topology, but not pixel-wise reconstruction, we also compare the results in terms of warping error Jain et al. (2010). The warping error

Table 1 Warping error on a testing set for one-section segmentation, segmentation based on three consecutive sections and for SUPERSLICING. Our method outperforms the baseline methods by 17 and 11%, respectively

Method	Warping error
One-section segmentation (Kaynig et al. 2010)	$2.876 * 10^{-3}$
Three consecutive sections (Laptev et al. 2012)	$2.693 * 10^{-3}$
SuperSlicing segmentation	$2.384 * 10^{-3}$

measures the topological error between proposed labeling $\hat{X}$ and a reference labeling $X^\star$. It is evaluated as squared Euclidean distance between $X^\star$ and the "best warping" F of $\hat{X}$ onto $X^\star$ such that the warping F is from the class Λ that preserve topological structure: $\min_{F \in \Lambda} \sum_p \delta(F(\hat{X})_p, X_p^\star)$. For further information about the warping error the interested reader is referred to Jain et al. (2010). The results are summarized in Table 1. The results on sub-frame stack produced by SUPERSLICING are 17% better than one sections segmentation and 11% better then the results based on three neighboring sections.

5.2 Natural Videos

Rotating Fan We test the proposed algorithm on a rotating fan video from Shahar et al. (2011) to evaluate our method qualitatively.[2] As the rotation speed is higher than the shutter speed the frame renders blurred fan blades. Based on three neighboring frames and no prior information we estimate $L = 3$ hidden sub-frames with linear interpolation, optical flow interpolation and the proposed method. Figure 6 shows the results of comparison. As can be seen linear interpolation blurs sub-frames even more. Optical flow interpolation shows the rotation of the fan, but as the initial frames are blurred, the resulting warping is blurred as well. SUPERSLICING shows superior results: it reconstructs the original shape of the blades and renders sharp sub-frames.

KTH dataset We perform synthetic experiments on the KTH action database Schuldt et al. (2004) to quantify the quality of SUPERSLICING's reconstruction. This database consists of videos recorded at 24 frames per second. We first downsample the frame rate to 8 frames per second while taking an average of three neighboring frames (low frame rate videos). Then we reconstruct sub-frames with four different methods: frame repetition, linear interpolation, optical flow warping and SUPERSLICING. Figure 7 shows qualitative results for the number of hidden sub-frames equal $L = 2$ or 3. Boxplots in Fig. 8 visualises the comparison of peak signal to noise ratio (PSNR) evaluated on 25 frames of video for $L = 3$ and $L = 2$ respectively. SUPERSLICING outperforms baseline methods for almost all frames and the average quantitative

---

[2]We do not compare with Shahar et al. (2011) directly, as their method operates under different assumptions and, moreover, they provide no quantitative results.

Fig. 6 A comparison of SUPERSLICING with the results of alternative methods. Column **a** shows original frames Y^1, Y^2 and Y^3. Each following column shows three interpolated frames estimated with: linear interpolation (**b**), optical flow warping (**c**), SUPERSLICING (**d**). *Arrows* point out that SUPERSLICING results in less blurred fan blades

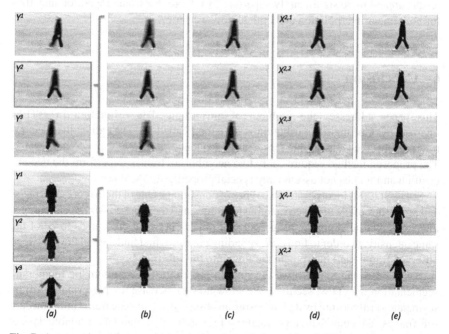

Fig. 7 A comparison of our reconstruction results with the results of different methods and with ground truth. *Top* walking person video reconstruction with $L = 3$ hidden sub-frames. *Bottom* hand waving person video reconstruction with $L = 2$ hidden sub-frames. Column **a** shows original frames Y^1, Y^2 and Y^3 from low frame rate video. Three following column shows $L = 3$ interpolated frames estimated with: linear interpolation (**b**), optical flow warping (**c**), SUPERSLICING (**d**). Column **e** shows ground truth from high frame rate video. Our results are less blurred and they are qualitatively closer to the ground truth than the results of the baseline methods

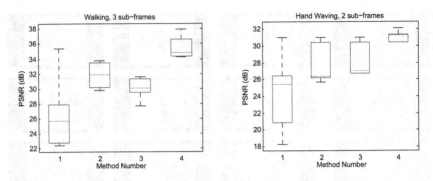

Fig. 8 An illustration of quantitative results on KTH videos for different methods. *Left plot* walking person video with $L = 3$ hidden sub-frames, *right plot* hand waving person video with $L = 2$ hidden sub-frames. Each boxplot shows statistics for PSNR (in dB) evaluated for: frame repetition (**1**), linear interpolation (**2**), optical flow warping (**3**) and our method (**4**)

results appear to be significantly superior: 23% better for frame repetition and 10% for both linear interpolation and optical flow warping.

6   Conclusion

This paper addresses the problem of anisotropic data restoration in ssTEM microscopy. Our main contribution is a method called SUPERSLICING that decomposes an observed anisotropic frame into a sequence of *hidden isotropic sub-frames*. The proposed method requires only two neighboring frames to perform the decomposition and it does not assume any special properties of the data.

SUPERSLICING incorporates two types of constraints. One of them represents physical properties of the involved imaging technique and the other constraint encourages the pixels that lie along the progression of objects between the frames to be of the same intensity. In order to find corresponding pixels we first find optical flow between observed frames and interpolate the flow into the sub-frames.

Based on SUPERSLICING we develop an algorithm for an automatic membrane segmentation in ssTEM sections. We show how to increase the performance of the segmentation algorithm by decomposing an observed anisotropic frame into isotropic sub-frames. We demonstrate the quality of the method on publicly available dataset where it performs, in term of warping error, 17 and 11% better than the baselines.

We also provide both qualitative and quantitative results for videos from the KTH action video dataset. We artificially synthesize blurred low frame rate video and decompose it into sub-frames. We evaluate PSNR and compare the results with three different baseline methods. Our results are on average 10% better than state-of-the-art.

Acknowledgements This work was partially supported by the SNF grant Sinergia CRSII3_130 470/1.

References

S. Baker, D. Scharstein, J. P. Lewis, S. Roth, M. J. Black, and R. Szeliski. A database and evaluation methodology for optical flow. *International Journal of Computer Vision*, 92:1–31, 2011.

L. Breiman. Random forests. *Machine Learning*, 45(1):5–32, 2001.

A. Cardona and S. Saalfeld et al. An integrated micro- and macroarchitectural analysis of the drosophila brain by computer-assisted serial section electron microscopy. *PLoS Biol*, 10, 2010.

T. Hu and J. Nunez-Iglesias et al. Super-resolution using sparse representations over learned dictionaries: Reconstruction of brain structure using electron microscopy. *CoRR*, abs/1210.0564, 2012.

V. Jain and B. Bollmann et al. Boundary learning by optimization with topological constraints. In *CVPR*, pages 2488–2495, 2010.

V. Kaynig, T. J. Fuchs, and J. M. Buhmann. Geometrical consistent 3d tracing of neuronal processes in sstem data. In *MICCAI 2010*, pages 209–216. Springer Berlin / Heidelberg, 2010.

D. Laptev, A. Vezhnevets, S. Dwivedi, and J. M. Buhmann. Anisotropic sstem image segmentation using dense correspondence across sections. In *MICCAI*, pages 323–330, 2012.

D. Laptev, A. Vezhnevets, and J. M. Buhmann. Superslicing frame restoration for anisotropic sstem. In *IEEE 11th International Symposium on Biomedical Imaging ISBI 2014*. IEEE Xplore, 2014.

D. G. Lowe. Object recognition from local scale-invariant features. In *ICCV*, pages 1150–. IEEE, 1999.

K. Sandberg and M. Brega. Segmentation of thin structures in electron micrographs using orientation fields. *Journal of Structural Biology*, 157(2):403–415, 2007.

Christian Schuldt, Ivan Laptev, and Barbara Caputo. Recognizing human actions: A local svm approach. In *ICPR*, 2004.

S. Seung. Connectome: How the brain's wiring makes us who we are. *Houghton Mifflin Harcourt*, 2012.

Oded Shahar, Alon Faktor, and Michal Irani. Space-time super-resolution from a single video. In *CVPR*, pages 3353–3360, 2011.

M. Shimano, T. Okabe, I. Sato, and Y. Sato. Video temporal super-resolution based on self-similarity. In *ACCV*, pages 93–106, 2010.

Appendix A
Supplemental Information

Editors: Demian Battaglia, Isabelle Guyon, Vincent Lemaire, Javier Orlandi, Bisakha Ray, Jordi Soriano

Appendix I: Challenge Website
The above link points to the website of the first connectomics challenge we organized on Kaggle to reconstruct neuronal connectivity from calcium fluorescence recordings.

Appendix II: Data
[Data mirror [Kaggle (Chicago data center)]]
[Data mirror [Causality Workbench (ETH, Zurich)]]

Appendix III: Results Table
The results table contain a snapshot of the Kaggle leaderboard showing the ranking of the participants.
[Download paper describing design of challenge from the workshop held at IEEE IJCNN 2014]
[Download technical report from the workshop held at ECML 2014]

Appendix IV: Challenge Verification
This webpage describes the challenge verification.

© Springer International Publishing AG 2017
D. Battaglia et al. (eds.), *Neural Connectomics Challenge*, The Springer Series
on Challenges in Machine Learning, DOI 10.1007/978-3-319-53070-3

Printed in the United States
By Bookmasters